AN IMPROBABLE GIFT OF BLESSING

# An Improbable Gift of Blessing

## Prayers to Nurture the Spirit

❖ ✄ ❖

MAREN C. TIRABASSI AND
JOAN JORDAN GRANT

UNITED CHURCH PRESS
Cleveland, Ohio

United Church Press, Cleveland, Ohio 44115

© 1998 by Maren C. Tirabassi and Joan Jordan Grant

Printed in the United States of America on acid-free paper

03  02  01  00  99  98      5  4  3  2  1

LIBRARY OF CONGRESS CATALOGING-IN-PUBLICATION DATA

Tirabassi, Maren C.
    An improbable gift of blessing : prayers and affirmations to nurture the spirit /
    Maren C. Tirabassi and Joan Jordan Grant.
        p.      cm.
    Includes indexes.
    ISBN 0-8298-1220-2 (pbk. : alk. paper)
    1. Worship programs.  2. Church year.  I. Grant, Joan Jordan.
    BV30.T57  1997                                                97-33604
    242'.3—dc21                                                    CIP

# Contents

# Words from the Authors

◈ ✄ ◈

Reflecting on the lectionary scripture for the fourth Sunday in Advent, Year A, we wrote this prayer:

> As we ponder why we should be so honored by your gift,
> leap forth with joy from the ocean of birth within.
> Incarnate us to be your improbable gift of blessing to another,
> for you have believed in us, that we might bring to completion
> your promise of radical love to the whole world.

*An Improbable Gift of Blessing* is a diary of prayer. In it, we invite readers into a process of engagement with the Scriptures—a process which has nurtured us in our pastoring, spiritual direction, workshop leadership, and private devotional practice. We offer both a resource book and a welcome to read, rest, and pray Scripture.

## THE SHAPE OF *An Improbable Gift of Blessing*
### Scripture Sections

We have chosen forty-eight combinations of two to four scriptures. Most are lectionary selections and are so identified at the end of each section. Some texts are chosen across the lectionary grain in order to celebrate nonlectionary texts (and nonlectionary churches!). There is an even dispersion among the three years and throughout the church seasons. The book begins with the first week in Advent.

Each Scripture section approaches the Scripture in four ways: a Prayer of the Heart, Bible Study, Resources for Congregational Worship, and a Prayer beyond the Church. Although each of these independently relates to one or more of the texts in the chosen set of scriptures, there is a progression from interior reflection through the expanding contexts of a small study group, a congregation, and the larger community and world. Because too much symmetry is unrealistic (at least for us), some of the Scripture sections include more than one Prayer of the Heart, Bible Study activity, or Prayer beyond the Church.

## Prayer of the Heart

All prayer is rooted in a personal experience with the scripture text. We ask readers to begin by reading the scripture, and we then share a related prayer that is particular to our spiritual journey. We hope this will serve as a window into the text from which each reader will reflect on his or her own internal understanding of the scripture and will deepen his or her own prayer.

## Bible Study

Each Bible Study has two distinct parts.

The Creative Encounter with the Text for a Small Group is an experiential exercise, a stretching of the spiritual imagination. These use more than verbal exchanges. Participants are invited to draw maps, mold clay, drink water from communion cups, plant seeds, eat together, light candles, and go outside for a walk. This is an "encounter" with Scripture particularly accessible to those who do not learn "wordwise," but also an opportunity for highly verbal participants to be caught off-guard by God.

Questions for Discussion or Personal Reflection are shaped to engage a person's life immediately with the scripture text rather than reflect on its historical associations. Some groups may want to preface this discussion with textual scholarship. The questions are not numbered and do not need to be completed like a study guide. They suggest several points of beginning, and most groups will focus intensively on only one or two. We usually conclude a class that uses questions like these by encouraging the participants to create a prayer together that touches the issues raised by the discussion.

## Resources for Congregational Worship

We have included calls to worship, invocations, and confessional sequences (Time of Reconciliation) based on the chosen texts. Permission to copy these—as well as other materials in the book—is freely given for church bulletins, newsletters, and congregational and educational use, with appropriate acknowledgment.

Reprinting these resources in other forms (such as a book or for a workshop for which a fee is charged) requires the additional permission of the United Church Press. The liturgical resources and Bible Study materials may be adapted, but the Prayers of the Heart and Prayers beyond the Church require the authors' permission (usually very willingly given) for alteration.

## Prayers beyond the Church

In various stages of the manuscript preparation these prayers have been called "Prayers of the World" and "Contemporary Prayers." We returned to the original title because it seemed to say—simply, if awkwardly—what we wanted to do: to pray a bridge from the Scripture to an issue of contemporary relevance. We entered into each text seeking metaphors honest enough to be understood as clearly at the truck stop, on the Internet, and in the prison cell as in the narthex. Some of these prayers are for professions, and some reflect life situations. We did not create a list of socially relevant concerns and then search for Scripture to speak to them, but listened long and hard to the scripture until it spoke—to careers as diverse as construction, advertising, and intensive care, and to issues as diverse as anorexia, assisted suicide, and new relationships after divorce. A woman asked us on a recent evening if we had a prayer for physical and occupational therapists. We don't . . . yet. There are so many professions and concerns that we haven't even begun to pray.

## Ember Days

*An Improbable Gift of Blessing* presents a year with four seasons of prayer each including twelve Scripture sections. These seasons are based on the four Ember Days, a quarterly observance of many traditions which probably originated with a harvest cycle. Ember Day observance of Wednesday, Friday, and Saturday four times a year as a "small Lent"—a time of pausing, reflection, and prayer—begins on the Wednesdays occurring after the First Sunday in Lent, after Pentecost, after September 14, and after December 13.

## The Drawings

We have marked each of the Ember Days with a drawing, an opportunity for the reader to pause and pray in a way that is beyond words. It was late in our work together when we realized that the drawings for the book needed to be of benches—places to rest along the journey of our lives through the year. These benches are our offering of incarnate Sabbath. We invite you to pray them, as we invite you to be in Sabbath in this diary of prayer. These particular benches were chosen to reflect the Ember Days. The "Sources of Inspiration for the Drawings" is on page 221.

# Ways to Use *An Improbable Gift of Blessing*

The Resources for Congregational Worship can easily be transferred to worship services, and the Questions for Discussion and Personal Reflection used for sermon preparation or Bible study classes. A single question can be a line in a church bulletin or the introduction to the reading of Scripture in a worship service. The Creative Encounters with the Text work well in adult Bible studies, confirmation classes, workshops, and retreats. They may also be used to create contexts for alternative worship services. The Prayers of the Heart can be used devotionally or as bulletin reflections. There is a separate index for the Prayers beyond the Church to cross-reference the issues and professions that are raised. These concerns may be the focus of an ecumenical service, a conference, or a seminar, during which the prayers may be used.

Although the immediate usefulness of *An Improbable Gift of Blessing* for Bible study and Sunday morning worship is obvious, it is important that these "church times" be grounded in both an intense personal encounter with Scripture and a listening to that scripture's call to be engaged with the secular world—with the pain and struggle and the joy and doubt and loneliness and injustice that are reality. Providing all four dimensions for each scripture emerges from an internal integrity. Several of those who have read the manuscript have used it as a private devotional guide. They have read the scripture each day of the week, and on the first day focused on the Prayer of the Heart. For each of the next four days they chose a single question for reflection. On the sixth day they read the Prayer beyond the Church. On the seventh day they wrote a personal prayer, either a Prayer of the Heart or a Prayer beyond the Church. While the Resources for Congregational Worship were intended for group or church use, one reader found the Time of Reconciliation sequences a fulfilling part of his personal prayer exploration.

Although this is a book of prayer rather than a book about how to create prayer, our intention is to invite all readers into a rhythm of approaching Scripture in a fourfold manner, which can begin with the particular texts chosen here and continue as a study of any other passage of Scripture. We hope that those who use this book as a resource for planning Bible studies, workshops, seminars, and alternative worship services will be inspired by it to prepare their own multidimensional, integrated engagements with prayer and Scripture for the groups with whom they are working.

# *Words of Gratitude*

❖ ✄ ❖

## MANY PEOPLE ARE A PART OF THIS BOOK

Carole C. Carlson brought us together and suggested we share our worship resources. Her prayer and advice have sustained this project throughout every passage. She has been most honest, helpful, and creative with her suggestions. Many prayers were changed because of her comments or written because she missed them. Carole loved this book into being.

Several others read the manuscript and spent time with us—commenting, nudging, demanding clarification, and even pointing out comma errors. We thank Kathy Musser, Stephen Price, Philip J. Mayher, Hal Harrison, Susan Gregory-Davis, and Pat Parnell for the incredible amounts of time and care they gave this book.

Two groups of people worked with these materials and offered their unique perspectives. We are grateful to the New Hampshire Conference Interim Ministry Group and the Spirituality and Recovery Group of the Massachusetts Department of Corrections Intensive Treatment Program.

We have been nurtured during the time of writing this book by our congregations. Joan formerly served as pastor of spiritual formation and visitation at the Congregational Church of Hollis, New Hampshire. Currently she continues her ministry of spiritual direction and as a facilitator for retreats, workshops, and contemplative prayer groups. Maren was interim pastor at Dane Street Congregational United Church of Christ in Beverly, Massachusetts, when we began the book and is now pastor of the Northwood Congregational United Church of Christ in Northwood, New Hampshire. These congregations have been "called" to worship, assured of grace, questioned and experimented upon in Bible studies. Retreat groups from Wilbraham United Church of Christ in Wilbraham, Massachusetts, Wolfeboro Congregational United Church of Christ in Wolfeboro, New Hampshire, and Salem Tabernacle Church of Salem, Massachusetts, shared in the shaping of some Creative Encounters with the Text. The Salem folks proved Carole wrong—people older than youth *will* wrap up in toilet paper!

Our families have loved us through this process, as well as typing, reading, and being patient. Many thanks to Clair Grant and Don Tirabassi and our children, Ben Grant and Matthew and Maria Tirabassi.

Diane Karr, typist and friend, and a professional editor, has supported this book with her technical skills and spiritual insight. Without her, *An Improbable Gift of Blessing* not only wouldn't have been finished on time, it probably wouldn't have been finished at all.

Finally, we deeply appreciate Kim Sadler, our editor at United Church Press, for believing in this project, responding to our many questions, and offering the warmth of her friendship.

# Advent and Christmas

# Waking into Advent

(PSALM 80:1–7, 17–19; 1 CORINTHIANS 1:3–9;
MARK 13:24–37)

❖ ✄ ❖

## PRAYER OF THE HEART

### (MARK)

*"And what I say to you I say to all: Keep awake." (Mark 13:37)*

God, wake with me!
All this Advent scripture
is hard on insomniacs.
Startled from sleep
at three,
I wonder why I am
haunted by a sense
of something left
undone.

And then I remember—

This is Advent,
the solitary chewing
on the night,
the restive waiting with
the midnight taste
of half-said prayers
and memories.
This, this is Advent, too,
not just starlit scenes
in Christmas cards
and the soft story
dispensing traditional
comfort.

This is Advent—this
red-eyed wondering
about the meaning
of it all, this
red-eyed, lonely-pacing,
holy-hurting encounter
with the mirror
and You,
and every ill-spent
Advent past,
searching for the meaning,
for the meaning
of it all.

## BIBLE STUDY
## Creative Encounter with the Text for a Small Group
### *Waiting—Prayers for our Friends*
### (MARK)

Create a list of "waiting" situations. Some examples are: "My friend is waiting for a child to be born"; "My friend is waiting for mortgage approval"; "My friend is waiting for her husband to come out of surgery"; "My friend is waiting for a college acceptance"; "My friend is waiting to die." Cut them into strips of paper and put them in a grab bag. Each participant will draw one out and write a prayer of empathy by mentally entering into the situation of this imaginary friend. For people who have been through the situation, this may be an exercise in memory; for those who have a friend who is facing that kind of waiting, it will be an exercise of reality. In the sharing time, emphasize how many different times during our lives we are involved in waiting and yet how similar the emotions are. Discuss what it means to pray in intercession for people we know and for people whom we do not know personally.

## Suggested Questions for Discussion or Personal Reflection

### (PSALM 80:1–7, 17–19)

What prayers do you think make God angry?

Have you ever longed for God to be stirred up and act?

The psalm says, "save us." What is salvation for a group?

### I CORINTHIANS 1:3–9

What are spiritual gifts?

On what occasions do you give thanks to God for others?

For what revelation of God are you waiting?

Why does Advent matter this year?

### MARK 13:24–37

What do you expect of the Second Coming? Are you intrigued, repelled, frightened, or amused by churches that predict the end of the world? Why?

What is the power of apocalyptic speech?

How do we "keep awake" for God?

Would you rather focus your Advent worship on the Apocalypse or the Judean baby? Why?

# RESOURCES FOR CONGREGATIONAL WORSHIP

## Call to Worship

### (MARK)

Advent your lives. Be disturbed.

Wait and wait and wait and wait.

Suddenly, God is coming.

Keep awake, alert, uneasy, and alive.

## Invocation

### (I CORINTHIANS)

We give thanks, Emmanuel,

for the community of the faithful and for spiritual gifts found—

not under the tinsel-laden tree—

but in the hearts of friends.
Help us not only to light the candles and carol the traditions
of the Bethlehem revelation, but to wait
for the startling new revealing of Christ in our lives. Amen.

## Time of Reconciliation

(PSALMS)

### Call to Confession

Sometimes God is angry even with our prayers. Let us confess our sins.

### Confession

O God, we pray one-way prayers which allow no time for listening.
We seek favored status for ourselves, our families, our friends, our nation.
We try to manipulate you, bargain with you, control you, avoid you.
We pray Christmas holiness in our homes and churches,
　rather than opening a year-long room at the inn
　for the stranger, the lonely one, the child.
Restore us, O God.
Let us see ourselves in your shining face. Amen.

### Assurance of Grace

God restores us. God's face shines on us and we are saved.

## PRAYER BEYOND THE CHURCH

### Prayer with Lay Leaders

(I CORINTHIANS, MARK)

Some clergy think
they are in the
alarm-clock sermon
business,

but I believe that
caring for this church
is really about keeping
it awake—
in the evening
of pastoral transition
and the midnight
of congregational crisis,
at the cock crow
of the annual meeting
and the tired dawn
of one more fair,
church school teacher

recruitment,
diaconate meeting,
bathrobe pageant,
harvest supper,
prayer meeting,
Bible study, and
newsletter . . .

and it's about holding together
the spiritual gifts
of the choir and
the quilters, the
five-year-olds and the
nonagenarians,
the steeple-lovers
and the pigeon-table
overturners,
the folks who are

almost bored
by a life of
being faithful
and the ones trying
to find a way back
to a place in the pew
they ran away from
long ago . . .

and it's about showing
in my life just how
wonderful
the watching is—
the watching

for a Christmas
that didn't just happen
long ago
in a manger in a cave,
but is going to come
suddenly—
any hour—
in the flesh of folks
who are just like
you and me,
waiting for some
hope, guiding stars
and glory.

The preceding materials use some of the lectionary readings for the First Sunday in Advent, Year B.

# Welcomed and Prepared

(ISAIAH 11:1–10; ROMANS 15:4–13; MATTHEW 3:1–12)

❖ ✿ ❖

## Prayer of the Heart
### (MATTHEW)

*"'Repent, for the [realm] of heaven has come near.'"(Matthew 3:2)*

O preparing God,

Send me this day, a messenger
to prepare a way for you in me.
Send me, this day, an angel
for the covenant you expect me to honor.
Send me, this day, a voice
calling me to repentance.
Send me, this day, a friend
to love me with the breath of your passion.

Call me out from self-justifying barriers.
Call me down from self-promoting pedestals.
Call me up from self-defeating prostrations.
Call me into your wilderness
where I may find your forgiveness.

Return me to my center where you live.
Set my senses firmly on your truth
which is written on my heart
and yet needs another to
cry it out to me.
Ready my expectations that you will come—
    come to the meal of my wild honey,
    come to the bathing of my dark river,
    come to the harvest of threshed words
    with fork and fire and Spirit—
when I trust you to prepare my impossibilities
to receive you as living flesh.
Amen.

# BIBLE STUDY
## Creative Encounter with the Text for a Small Group
### Biography of the Baptist
#### (MATTHEW)

Prepare a biography of John the Baptist. Collect the scriptures that describe the prophecy of his birth, his mother's pregnancy and the visit from her cousin, his birth, his ministry and encounter with Jesus, his relationship to his own disciples, the inquiries he sent to Jesus, and his death. We usually experience these pieces throughout the year as they relate to Jesus' life. Working together, develop from them, and any secondary references available, a portrait of this strange lonely man, so that he can be honored by the group in this season of preparation.

## Suggested Questions for Discussion or Personal Reflection
### (ISAIAH 11:1–10)

Justice advocates and ecology advocates are often in conflict. How does this passage interconnect these two issues?

Why does true justice for the poor sometimes involve more than immediate sensory evidence?

What is your favorite image of creation peacefulness in this passage? Why?

### (ROMANS 15:4–13)

How do we welcome one another? What constitutes "welcome"?

In what ways can Scripture be used to give people hope and encouragement?

What do the words "Jews and Gentiles" mean to you?

What is/should be the relationship of contemporary Judaism and Christianity?

### (MATTHEW 3:1–12)

How do you feel about "reformers"—particularly if they dress in unusual fashion and are verbally critical of institutions?

What is repentance? What feelings or actions are involved in it? (Remorse, confession, reconciliation, penance, restitution are possibilities.)

Who has "prepared" you for God?

# RESOURCES FOR CONGREGATIONAL WORSHIP
## Call to Worship
### (ISAIAH)

O Root of Jesse, come and save us.


O Wolf-tamer and Leopard-gentler,
come and touch us tenderly.

O Sower of the field where cow and bear graze,
   where calf and cub play together,
   come and teach us love across diversity.

O Lover of serpents and children,
   come and draw the poison out of our family relationships.

O One of many antiphons, who names us naming you,
   come and in-spirit us
   against hurt and destroying,
   in counsel and might,
   for wisdom and understanding
   through fear and delight.

## Invocation

### (ROMANS)

Emmanuel, we praise you for welcoming us into God's presence. Help us in this hour to welcome one another fully and wondrously. And may the God of hope fill us with all joy and peace in believing, so that we may abound in hope by the power of the Holy Spirit. Amen.

## Time of Reconciliation

### (MATTHEW)

### *Call to Confession*

Advent calls all of us into the wilderness of self-reflection.

### *Confession*

O God, we offer you our repentance.
We replace holy days with holidays.
We hurry past opportunities to give the
   gifts of kindness and honesty,
We do not prepare the place
   for your birth in our lives.
We do not listen to angels in our dreams,
   forgive those dearest to us,
   or welcome into hearts and homes,
   the poor and the stranger.
Accept our humility and guide us to your grace. Amen.

### *Assurance of Grace*

True confession is received with complete forgiveness. In our gratitude we bear the fruit of repentance.

# Prayer Beyond the Church

*Prayer with the Environment*

(ISAIAH)

Dolphins shall not be strangled by plastic
nor cormorants covered in oil.
Coyotes shall not be sport-killed
nor sled-dogs tormented.
Red woods shall not be felled,
chickens penned, mink and fox
harvested for fur.
Eagles shall not fly with no
place for a nest.
People will respect the snakes
and learn to understand
the spirits of vultures
and weasels. Children
will sit on the warmth of rocks
and find the balsams
in the forest
more beautiful than the
Christmas trees
in the entrance to the mall.
Adults will walk the ocean beach,
and they will not find
the ritual circle of
beer can trash.

The peace between creatures
will be bloody when people
do not disturb the
balance of predator and prey,
and people will look in themselves
and discover
that they are kin
to the wolf and lamb
and the turtle and the wind,
the sand by the sea and
even the cancer cell.
God will be found in roots
and peace on earth
will be an angel song
made soil, and

we will not hurt or destroy
in all the mountains and suburbs,
the barrios and farm fields,
the oil wells and outbacks and
fishing banks, for we will be filled
with the knowledge of our own
holiness, as the Spirit
covers the sea.

The preceding materials use some of the lectionary readings for the Second Sunday in Advent, Year A.

*Welcomed*
*and Prepared*

# Stirring the Spirit

## (ISAIAH 61:1–4, 8–11; 1 THESSALONIANS 5:16–24)

### PRAYER OF THE HEART
#### (1 THESSALONIANS)

*"Do not quench the Spirit." (1 Thessalonians 5:19)*

I will not quench the Spirit
with fruitcake and cookies,
mistletoe and presents,
parties and poinsettias,
firelight and pine.

I will not quench the Spirit
with eggnog and memories,
tinsel and wrappings,
Amahl and O'Henry,
Nutcracker and Scrooge.

I will not quench the Spirit
with greeting cards and wassail,
reindeer and Bing Crosby,
snowfall and sleigh rides,
solstice and dark.

I will not quench the Spirit
even with Advent wreath,
manger-words, angel-song,
even with pageants
and Magi-stars, with the
running of shepherds,
and the fearful hopes
of all the years,
even with caroling
in nursing homes
and toys given to children
who are poor,
even with Christmas Eve
midnight, candleshine
and prayer.

I will not quench the Spirit—
I will be still
in the presence
of birth.

## BIBLE STUDY
### Creative Encounter with the Text for a Small Group
#### Garland
##### (ISAIAH)

Bring in a large evergreen wreath and ribbons of medium-width cut in pieces. Have the participants identify the oppressed, brokenhearted, captives, and prisoners. Take the time to make a significant list inclusive of personal, interpersonal, community, and global possibilities. Write each one on a piece of ribbon and tie them on the wreath to make a garland of the good news. Have the participants plan a way to share the wreath with the rest of the congregation.

# Winter Ember Days

"And Jesus said to his disciples, 'Sit here while I pray.'" (Mark 14:32b)

# Suggested Questions for Discussion or Personal Reflection
## (ISAIAH 61:1–4, 8–11)

What would a spirit of anointing mean in this year?

What particular "good news" for the oppressed can you identify this Advent season?

What is a "garland of gladness" for you?

What does it feel like to mourn in the midst of holiday preparations?

What is comfort in Advent?

What is in ruin in our cities? How can ruins be repaired?

## (1 THESSALONIANS 5:16–24)

What does the concept "pray without ceasing" mean to you?

In the midst of seasonal festivity, what keeps your body sound? What keeps your soul (psyche) sound? What keeps your spirit sound?

What is attacking your body, soul, and spirit?

Can you rejoice always and give thanks in all circumstances? Give an example of a thankless circumstance.

Tell a story of an Advent or Christmas when you truly felt Jesus Christ had come. What happened which made you know Christ's presence?

# RESOURCES FOR CONGREGATIONAL WORSHIP
## Call to Worship
### (1 THESSALONIANS)

**One voice:** In this season of holiness we pause.

**Congregation:** We stand under the light of the star and feel it illuminate the corners of our lives.

**One voice:** We will not treat Advent as a census, counting off days and things to be done.

**Congregation:** We will enter the circle of the silence—where body, soul, and spirit are embraced by the wild peace of Christ's coming.

## Invocation

Lean down to us an angel,
light a star,
kindle a Christmas,
manger us your peace,
and whisper in us the name of love.

## Time of Reconciliation
### (ISAIAH 61)

### Call to Confession

We have held fingers over the good news on our lips—
willing the gospel to be a comfort-contract

not a covenant with justice.
Let us confess our sins.

## Confession

Emmanuel, peaceful one, prophet-spoken—
We have avoided the oppressed,
     blamed the captives,
     forgotten the prisoners,
     and have not opened our broken hearts
          for fear of losing the pieces.
Repair the ruined places in our lives with repentance,
     restoration and hope. Amen.

## Assurance of Grace

We are the people of faint spirit who are offered a chance to praise.
We are the ones with Spirit on our heads
     who can proclaim the year of God's favor.

## PRAYER BEYOND THE CHURCH

### Prayer with the City in Ruins

#### (ISAIAH)

Runaways and junkies
lean against street lamps
tarted up with red plastic bows
and silver garland,
tattered from blizzards past,
but still a sign of season.
And Salvation Army ringers
in blue-caped mantles of praise
bell mercy on the corners
in the snowfall, while
teenagers with no jobs,
lonely in the early dusk of
solstice and meaninglessness,
light a cigarette counterpoint
to solitary electric candles
which shine on the
eightieth Christmases
of poor old women
who live in single rooms.

On the Boston Common
every tree is crowned
with glittering bulbs
which give a few days'
merriment to sleepers
on the grates and benches.
All of these qualify
as the company of the
broken-hearted—
listening for angel wings,
not really expecting
any big stars anymore,
but waiting for anyone
with Spirit who is willing
to walk the streets
and talk some holy ragtime
tidings of comfort
and justice and peace—
and the possibility
of a really new year.

Anoint me.

The preceding materials use some of the lectionary readings for the Third Sunday in Advent,
Year B.

# The Power of Birth

## (MICAH 5:2–5A; LUKE 1:26–56)

❖ ✺ ❖

## PRAYER OF THE HEART

### (LUKE)

*"For nothing will be impossible with God." (Luke 1:37)*

O Blessing God,
I am immersed in your story.
I am Mary and Elizabeth;
I am prophet and singer,
old mother, fetus and angel,
and I know you.
You enter a woman and through her
you enter the human hearts
of all who eat the fruit of her womb.
You come to those who cannot trust
their own strength to live.
You find your way to me
through my most vulnerable need.

O Blessing God,

May the sound of greeting this day
cause the child within me
to leap with expectation,
and, as I ponder why I should be
so honored by your gift,
leap forth with joy from
the ocean of birth within.
Incarnate me to be your
improbable gift of blessing
to another,
for you have believed in me,
that I might bring to completion
your promise of radical love
to the whole world.
Amen.

## BIBLE STUDY

### Creative Encounter with the Text for a Small Group

*Option: Draw an Angel*

#### (LUKE)

Make time for meditation with soft music. Suggest a focus on angels—biblical images, personal experiences, popular literature, movie versions. Let people take ten minutes to meditate on angels and then ten more minutes to draw an angel. Share the drawings and any "angel stories" people have.

### *Option: Finding Mary*

#### (LUKE)

Protestants—for the most part—lost Mary during the Reformation. Bring in artistic images of Mary, including some with a diversity of racial and ethnic characteristics, and prayers to Mary from Roman Catholic and Eastern Orthodox sources. Discuss the various references to Mary in the Bible. Ask around the table what Mary has meant to the participants. Write a "prayer," a conversation with Mary, as either an individual or group exercise.

## Suggested Questions for Discussion or Personal Reflection
### (MICAH 5:2–5A)

What does Bethlehem mean to you?

What is peaceful world leadership?

Why do we read prophecy?

What do you think prophecy is?

Does Jesus fulfill the prophecies of Hebrew prophets?

Do you expect prophecy now?

### (LUKE 1:26–56)

Why do you think God chose Mary?

Why do you think Mary chose God?

Why does knowing about Elizabeth's miracle make it easier for Mary to accept her own?

What have angels asked you to do?

What has made "the child leap in your womb"? What has filled you with that kind of wild joy?

What are some possibilities for the relationships between old women and young women?

How does Mary's hymn turn the social order upside-down?

Why does Mary connect her own blessedness with the plight of the poor and powerless?

In what ways do you feel connected to the poor?

## RESOURCES FOR CONGREGATIONAL WORSHIP
## Call to Worship
### (MICAH, LUKE)

Come to worship where you may be troubled by angels.

Come to prayer where you may be unsettled by politics.

Come to the candlelight of traditions which light up the darkness of this winter solstice and come to the unpredictable pregnancy of the Spirit.

Come to flesh-talk and poverty-talk and labor-pains-talk and peace-talk.

Come to expect a miracle.

# Invocation

(LUKE)

Emmanuel, we are grateful that the story of your human birth embraces us and helps us to accept our own humanity and the humanity of all your children. We are blessed by the holiness of this time of waiting, feeling your presence within us as Mary did so long ago. Amen.

# Time of Reconciliation

(LUKE)

## *Call to Confession*

Mary's song connects us to all people, and we confess our complicity in social and global sin.

## *Confession*

Savior God, Holy One—
  The powerful are on thrones,
  and the rich still feast,
  while the poor and powerless
  are turned away empty.
  We have repeated words of prophecy
  but have not sung your blessings
  from our hearts.
  We have not decided
  whether we want to scatter the proud,
  or seek their privileges for ourselves.
Help us to follow your nativity into the world.   Amen.

## *Assurance of Grace*

Forgiveness is God's flesh. So is pain. Let us embrace the Incarnation.

# Prayer beyond the Church
## Prayer with Those Who Are Pregnant
### (Luke)

I feel vulnerable and awkward,
turned inward
with great joy at the
secret under my heart.

Planned child, conceived
the month I tossed the pills,
unplanned child of
a reckless night,
or child so hoped for
we took the temperature
of our hearts
for years.
Child of my childhood
or my old age,
first child or second child
or seventh,
body-carried birth or
heart-carried adoption—
it doesn't matter.
I am pregnant.

I am drawn into the
friendship of women,
recognizing our
special blessings,
murmuring greetings
of miracle
and revolution,
but I am also in a
relationship so intimate
that it cannot be shared,
with a Mystery,
with an overshadowing
Spirit who hushes
me to awe.

More full of power
than I have ever been—
as if my words could
change the world—
I am singing
the connection of
this child's birth
with justice for all children,
and healing and plenty.

I know my womb has met
an angel.

The preceding materials use some of the lectionary readings for the Fourth Sunday in
Advent, Year C.

# Pausing after Christmas

❖ ✃ ❖

## PRAYER OF THE HEART
### (ISAIAH)

*"For as the earth brings forth its shoots, and as a garden causes what is*

*sown in it to spring up . . ." (Isaiah 61:11a)*

Sweet-Winter-Rose God,
your house is filled with the scent of green.
Flower and fern adorn your table
with the splendid fragrance
of light-seeking blossom and leaf—
seed of the garden,
shoot of the earth.

Sweet-Winter-Rose God,
how exquisite is the garden of difference
that wafts beauty on each season's care.
What word do you give to counter our fear
that our differences tear us apart?

From their differences—
flower and fern compliment,
organ and flute, harp and
human voice make music
none could shape alone,
word and sacrament worship
in such a conjoining
that body and soul are made one,
and human traditions, languages,
colors of skin, textures of hair,
create beauty on the earth,
your holy garden.

Let righteousness and praise
always spring up from your

green-scented shoots,
and I will rejoice,
now, under the shadow
of your Nativity,
in the cross which is
the sweetest tree, the white rose—
the cross which intermingles
death with resurrection,
the newborn in winter
with the union
of all love.

## BIBLE STUDY
## Creative Encounter with the Text for a Small Group
### *Wedding Garland and Bridal Jewels*
#### (ISAIAH)

Wedding imagery is used throughout Scripture as a metaphor for human joy in relationship to God. Weddings are times of celebration and great hope. Discuss modern weddings—both the positive and negative aspects. Then draw up a list of wedding images—bridal gowns, photographers, many-tiered cakes, vows, music, toasts, gifts, dancing. Have each participant choose one image and use it in a brief paragraph as a metaphor for his or her feelings about God.

## Suggested Questions for Discussion or Personal Reflection
#### (ISAIAH 61:10–62:3)

What is planted in the garden of your life that needs to grow?

Consider people who are "clothed" by others—the very young, the very old, sick people, actors. How does it feel for us to be clothed by God?

Reflect on the contemporary restoration of Jerusalem. How is it a "crown of beauty" and how is it a "burning torch"?

Do we wear our faith like bridal finery?

#### (LUKE 2:22–40)

When do we listen to the testimony of wise and old men and women?

What are some blessed experiences in your life brought about by the powerful connection between older adults and children?

How is Christ's presence in our world both a "light of revelation" and a "soul-piercing sword"?

# Resources for Congregational Worship
## Call to Worship

**One voice:** We enter into worship under the light of God's star.

**Congregation:** We follow in the path of wandering seekers of long ago.

**One voice:** We have experienced Christmas, and now we must center its meaning in our lives.

**Congregation:** Our prayers, our songs, our hopes, even our fears are holy through God's gift of love.

## Invocation
### (LUKE)

Gentle God, the tinsel falls, the year turns, the carols fade. The blessing of Bethlehem that touched all the gray in our lives with star-silver is past. In this turning season of long cold nights, we ask God's presence beyond our holidays into the wintering times of our lives, so that we can begin to grow and become strong, filled with wisdom and the favor of God. Amen.

## Time of Reconciliation
### (LUKE)

### *Call to Confession*

We are more prone to confessing our seasonal excesses than our failure to experience incarnation fully. Let us pray.

### *Confession*

Emmanuel, God-with-us every day, we confess our sins:

We let the Christmas moment become the past in our lives.

We miss the holiness of children and the wisdom of old people.

We stop expecting miracles and Messiah.

We are so afraid to welcome death that we do not embrace life.

Reveal your salvation in us so that we may have peace.   Amen.

### *Assurance of Grace*

The good tidings are that God comes to us even when we are not looking. Accept your forgiveness. Be in peace.

# PRAYER BEYOND THE CHURCH
## Prayer with Grandparents and Other Aged Blessers

(LUKE)

We understand Christmas—
we know it better
for having seen it come
so many times,
with its sweet carols
and tinseled festivity,
with joy and hurry
and loneliness,
the unwrapping of gifts
which will be forgotten
so quickly, while
the memory of givers
will linger all the year.

We understand children—
we know them better
for having come to an age
when they matter more
and matter less to us.
We know how precious
it is to hold any child.
We care about unrelated children—
caroling on our doorsteps,
offering to shovel our snow,
making noise and fuss
in our nursing homes,
and those hurt or abandoned,
lost or refugeed
on our televisions.

And, ah, grandchildren.
We weekend them
with more pleasure
and are content
to send them home.
We can push a swing,
play Go Fish, tell stories,
and eat ice cream

longer than their parents.
We need naps, too.
We don't mind rock music
in small doses,
orange hair, peculiar
friends wearing
chains and pierced
in amazing places.
We will always bake cookies
or buy cookies
and sit at a kitchen table
and just listen
and listen,
and not judge.

We understand Christmas—
not the children's holiday
but the moment of hope
that we interpret
because the Holy Spirit
nests in our
gray hair and wrinkles,
replacement joints,
eyes with a trace
of glaucoma, and
wise old hands.
Each child is holy;
all parents need to be blessed
for the wonder and crosses
in their future, and,
because we hear salvation
in every newborn cry,
and recognize the
birth of God
in all toddlers and
teenagers,
we can welcome in peace
the someday-coming
of our own death.

The preceding materials use some of the lectionary readings from the First Sunday after Christmas, Year B.

# Epiphany

# Chosen in the Wilderness

## (ISAIAH 42:1–9; PSALM 29; MATTHEW 3:13–17)

❖ ✄ ❖

### PRAYER OF THE HEART
#### (ISAIAH)

*"Here is my servant, whom I uphold, my chosen in whom my soul delights." (Isaiah 42:1)*

Releasing God—
exiles, we are removed from the tents
of your indwelling peace.
Carried off by our postholiday,
midwinter, light-depriving captors:
letdown, fatigue, depression,
loneliness, inertia.

Releasing God—
We turn to you
for we remember your power.
We remember who creates the heavens
and who shapes the earth,
who breathes life into people
and all creatures.
We remember your name.
We remember that your
Word comes true.
We want you.
We are sorry when we forget to say it.

Releasing God—
How often you send us
what we don't expect.
A servant comes.
A servant—
in whom you delight,
wrapped in your own Spirit,
quiet, without shouting,
interior without persona,
gentle to the bruised,
patient with the wavering,
a servant of faithfulness and truth,
coming to lead us back.

Releasing God—
help us to find that your servant
lives within us, each one of us,
Help us to free that servant
to teach release to others.
Help us to be your servant lamp
that shines Love's freeing light
to all who lie in bondage.
Help us to be a releasing people
who find our servant selves
are at last home in the tent
of your in-dwelling peace.

# Prayer of the Heart

## (Matthew)

*"John would have prevented him, saying, 'I need to be baptized by you, and do you come to me?' But Jesus answered him, 'Let it be so now for it is proper for us in this way to fulfill all righteousness.' Then he consented."*
*(Matthew 3:14–15)*

As long as there have been gardens, there have been deserts.
Have you not created moist green and parched brown alike?
Out of your infinite wisdom come the fragrant balsam
and the prickly unkempt thorn bush.

You do not delight in your aromatic wonder
and disdain your outspoken bramble.
Birthed in soil and bent by wind,
you have invested as much spirit and truth
in the branches of one as the thick tangle of the other.

From the heart of the sweet-scented fir tree in the garden
do you not whisper unmistakably
your tidings of good news renewed?
Thus in the center of our own sweet-scented relationships in truth
is revealed your promise of love incarnate?

From out of the unruly thorn bush in the desert
Are you not crying out to us, each one of us,
by name, to turn to you?
So wildly do you venture to fail as a prophetic voice,
when we choose to not hear and change our ways.

O Proclaiming God—
moisten us by the message of your evergreen
source of mercy and love.
Sting us with the discomforting barbs of your personal call to repent.
Keep your voice alive
in the garden and the desert of our lives.
Proclaim your everlasting truth to us through the balsam
and through the briar.

# Bible Study
## Creative Encounter with the Text for a Small Group
### Remembering Baptism
#### (matthew)

In the center of your gathering, place a container of water—a font if you wish—with a rubber ducky floating in it. The image is baptism as the "childhood sacrament." Pass the rubber ducky around, and as each person holds it, have the participants tell a baptismal story—about their own baptisms or their children's baptisms, a service of baptismal renewal, or a baptism they watched as a congregational member. Duplicate the prayers (not the promises) from several different baptismal services. Use both prayers over the water and prayers for the person baptized or parents. Discuss the different themes of remembering, commitment, blessing, etc., in these prayers. Finally ask everyone to write a baptismal prayer for themselves. Leave the definition loose, allowing them to reflect on the stories, themes and images that have been raised. Ask those who are willing to share their prayers.

## Suggested Questions for Discussion or Personal Reflection
### (isaiah 42:1–9)

What does it mean to you to be God's servant?

God gives to people both "breath" and "spirit." What is the difference between breath and spirit?

Describe an experience in your life when you felt like a "dimly burning wick"?

What is ministry in prison?

### (psalm 29)

Name experiences of power in nature. Have you ever felt God in the midst of one of these?

Which of the images or metaphors in this psalm speaks to you? Why?

How do you worship God?

### (matthew 3:13–17)

Have you baptized Christ? What have you done for God or for people on God's behalf that seemed unnecessary or presumptuous?

What does baptism mean to you?

What is your clearest memory of baptism—of yourself, of one of your children, of someone else? Tell the story.

# Resources for Congregational Worship
## Call to Worship
(ISAIAH, PSALMS)

**One voice:** God creates the heavens and stretches them in sunset-crimson splendor and storm-purpled cloud.

**Congregation:** God spreads the earth with the blue and white of snow billows and the sun-gold of sparkling icicles.

**One voice:** Yet God breathes into every child the breath of life.

**Congregation:** And God fills with spirit all who walk the journey-path of life.

**One voice:** Let us worship God, who flings the silver of galaxies into deep space beyond time as we know it.

**Congregation:** Let us worship God, who calls us by name and holds our hands when we stumble.

## Invocation
(MATTHEW)

Why water, O God?
Why dove, fire, voice?
Why, when your Spirit comes,
are we surrounded by images?
Open us in this worship
to metaphor and grace.

## Time of Reconciliation
(ISAIAH)

### Call to Confession

We hear the cry—righteousness—not in the streets but in our hearts. We are uneasy.

### Confession

God who does not quench a dimly burning wick—
We repent the alternative values,
    the idols we serve instead of you.
We repent our turning away from kind words, just actions,
    whole and healing thoughts.
We repent our harsh judgment of others
    while excusing ourselves.
We repent our harsh judgment of ourselves
    which denies your desire to forgive.
God who does not break a bruised reed—
    accept our repentance.
Teach us how to be forgiven and responsible for new lives. Amen.

30

*Epiphany*

## Assurance of Grace

God has taken us by the hand and kept us. We are forgiven.

## PRAYER BEYOND THE CHURCH

*Prayer with People in Prison*

(ISAIAH, MATTHEW)

Fred, Cliff, Larry,
Doris, Frank, Mike,
Pete, Angela,
Micki, Elaine—
bruised reeds.
Ed, George, José,
Nate, Lisa,
Jahmal, Maria—
dimly burning wicks.
We are on Jordan's bank,
waiting for the baptism,
to name us all
with our own
beautiful names,
to open the sky
because we are
God's children.

It's not the submersion
part of baptism
that means so much.
Incarceration is what
we know too well—
crime and good time,

and the trap
and loneliness,
the hole, canteen,
and parole hearings,
life with miniature hopes,
sometimes no letters,
no visits,
sometimes fear. . . .
Yes, we understand drowning,
it's coming up
from the water
that's a miracle—

coming up sparkling
into some crazy
dove wings—
holy Lenny, Rosa,
holy Jones, Milt,
Abdoul—
called chosen servant,
named delightful and
beloved—and God
with us, too,
is well-pleased.

The preceding materials use some of the lectionary readings from the First Sunday after
Epiphany, Year A.

# Drinking the Revelation

## (ISAIAH 12; 1 CORINTHIANS 12:1–11; JOHN 2:1–11)

❖ ✄ ❖

## PRAYER OF THE HEART
### (ISAIAH)

*"With joy you will draw water from the wells of salvation." (Isaiah 12:3)*

Reassuring God,
to hearts of flesh that tremble,
so alike lost,
in valleys of despair,
to hearts of flesh that harden,
so alike lost,
in self-justifying pride,
to hearts of flesh dried up,
so alike lost,
in wastelands of success,
to hearts of flesh grown chill,
so alike lost,
in measuring how we love,
the invitation comes—
to draw water from the
wells of your salvation
in purest,
sweetest joy.

Reassuring God,
for every stream and spring
that wells up grace from deep

within your love,
I give my free and
heartfelt thanks.
The day has come,
when I draw forth rejoicing
the water of trust
and comfort,
from deep within your wells.
May all people
hear my thanks to you
resound in song.
May I hear my own voice,
glad with somersaulting
laughter
praise you for this
water-drawing,
feast-eating,
thanks-giving
day of days—
for I who would be
so lost, so lost,
am saved.

## BIBLE STUDY
### Creative Encounter with the Text for a Small Group

### *Option: Gifts of the Spirit*
#### (1 CORINTHIANS)

Gift-wrap small objects (bars of soap work well) and label them with the gifts of the Spirit listed in 1 Corinthians 12:1–11. Have several for each gift. Let each participant choose one that he or she has received or hopes to receive. Use the packages to visually cue the understanding that these are "gifts" and not "talents." Ask each person to share why he or she chose that particular gift.

### Option: A Toast
#### (JOHN)

Ask each participant to bring in one wine glass (a beautiful one). Switch them around and pour sparkling grape juice into them. Have each person share a memory from a wedding—his or her own or someone else's. Go around the circle a second time while each person makes a toast, until all the grape juice is gone.

## Suggested Questions for Discussion or Personal Reflection
### (ISAIAH 12)

For what do you give thanks to God in midwinter?
When have you had to draw on the "wells of salvation"—a deep place within yourself that knows you are saved, holy, precious?
Have you ever felt that God was angry with you? Why?

### (I CORINTHIANS 12:1–11)

What tests do you use to judge whether "the Spirit"—the enthusiasm, passion, religious faith—in a person is holy or unholy?
What is your gift of the Spirit? Begin by describing your personal characteristics and see if they combine to become one of the gifts mentioned in this passage.
Do you believe there is a hierarchy or an equality in gifts?
Which of the gifts in this passage do you not understand or would you not expect to find in a contemporary congregation?

### (JOHN 2:1–11)

Why does marriage need a miracle?
What does it mean that Jesus' first sign happened at a wedding?
Describe a day or an experience which was "just water" and changed amazingly into "wine"?

## RESOURCES FOR CONGREGATIONAL WORSHIP
## Call to Worship
### (ISAIAH, JOHN)

**One voice:** God invites us to come—
**Congregation:** and drink deeply of the wells of salvation.
**One voice:** God invites us to come—
**Congregation:** and drink lightly of the cup of celebration.
**One voice:** God invites us to come—

**Congregation:** We come with our thanksgiving and praise, with our inadequacy and need, seeking comfort for sadness, seeking a miracle for joy.

**One voice:** We are welcome.

**Congregation:** We need never thirst again.

## Invocation

O holy God, Architect of the cathedral of the winter-star-bright night and Embroiderer of the tiny crystal intimacy of the snowflake, we give you thanks and praise—

for your love and constancy in all seasons,
for the fires of romance, for the warmth of family,
for the glowing embers of aging, and
for the radiance of childhood eyes.

We kindle our lives with your precious Spirit and share that Spirit's spark with others we meet along these January days. Amen.

## Time of Reconciliation

### (1 CORINTHIANS)

### *Call to Confession*

The variety of religious experience often creates division and distrust rather than a Spirit-filled church.

Let us confess our sins.

### *Confession*

Gracious Spirit, you have given us gifts and we have misused them.

We ignore responsibilities inherent in our own spiritual gifts.
We envy some gifts and belittle others.
We are uncomfortable with the diversity of grace.
We sometimes discredit the spiritual expression of other Christians.

Return us to a clear focus on your compassion and power. Amen.

### *Assurance of Grace*

There is one Spirit—a Spirit of generosity and forgiveness. Thanks be to God.

## PRAYER BEYOND THE CHURCH

### *Prayer for New Relationships after Divorce*

### (JOHN)

After the wine ran out,
there was no wine,
there was no joy,
there was no dancing,
there was no party—

only six stone jars
of purification:
the deep jar of washing away
anger and ugly scenes;
the jar of parenting

that still flows between us
and we dip into
for grandparents
and college decisions,
and holiday bingo;
the bottle we filled up with tears,
and try-agains and counseling;
and the bucket
I splash over
my head in relief
that I'll never see
a courtroom again;
the cool cistern of
a new independence,
and finding out
who I really am;
and the buried cask
with the stone in its mouth
where I seal up
my sexuality.

But when I was just learning
to be thankful
for being water-rich,
someone crazy enough
to listen to angels and
believe in the
birth of God,
intervened and
decided
that my self-definition
as the person
where the wedding ran out,
wasn't complete.

No one leaves the
best wine for last,
they say.
Then, how could this
older, more vulnerable,
cracked-jar and broken-hope,
empty-wineskin
kind of person
be sipping a bouquet
of sweet promise and
intimacy rediscovered,
a slow vintage
for a celebration
that understands
the taste of regret
and still
drinks deeply
the cup of one another?

How could Cana
be the party where
divorced people come
to laugh?

Pass the water.
I want to toast this glass
so full of miracle
that the empty
and alone
that used to be me
will always be a sign
for everyone
of how much
God loves into all of us
a second chance
for loving.

The preceding materials use the Epistle and Gospel readings from the Second Sunday after Epiphany, Year C. The Hebrew Bible reading is found in the lectionary in both the Pentecost and Advent seasons in Year C.

# *Walking the Revelation*

## (MICAH 6:1–8; PSALM 15; I CORINTHIANS 1:18–30)

### PRAYER OF THE HEART
#### (MICAH, I CORINTHIANS)

*"And what does [God] require of you but to do justice, and to love kindness, and to walk humbly with your God?" (Micah 6:8b)*

The foolish cross
and the humble walk
I am seeking.
The broken strength
and the kind word
I am offering.
The divine controversy
and the wily debate
I am turning from.
The hard justice
and the shameful grace
I am learning.

In the avenue of stumbling blocks
I gladly journey—
because my feet are slow.
I am not weary of God
even in a wearied hour—
for my heart is slow.
I hear the call
of the not-powerful—
and my ears are slow.
I am not ashamed
of the Christ-story—
though my tongue is slow.

Accept my slow
following of you,
Yahweh of the just prophet,
Christ of the thorn-pricked saint.

Wake in me
a wounded listening.
Birth in me
a crazy boasting.
Heal me
with your foolish cross.
Walk with me
your humble walk.

## BIBLE STUDY
### Creative Encounter with the Text for a Small Group
### *Personal Life Maps*
#### (MICAH)

Invite each participant to draw a personal map of walking humbly with God.
They may respond to these thoughts:
Where does such a walk take you? Draw or name the places.
Who is willing to go with you? Name the people and put them beside the road.
What are the roadblocks? Draw them. Draw what gets around, under, or over
them.
What grows along the path? Do you see wildlife, birds? Are you in a city?
How do you feel on this walk?
Ask each participant to share some portion of his or her map with the group.

### Suggested Questions for Discussion or Personal Reflection
#### (MICAH 6:1–8)

What are God's controversies with people?
What are examples of doing justice?
What are examples of loving kindness?
What are examples of walking humbly with God?

#### (PSALM 15)

Is it always right to speak truth?
What is wrong with lending at interest or taking bribes (it's done all the time
in the contemporary corporate world)?
Why is just human interaction the criterion for dwelling in the tent of God?

#### (1 CORINTHIANS 1:18–31)

Are wisdom and faith opposites?
Why does God choose the foolish, weak, low, and despised in the world?
What is foolish in the message of the cross?

# RESOURCES FOR CONGREGATIONAL WORSHIP
## Call to Worship
### (1 CORINTHIANS)

**One voice:** God calls the simple, the weak, the powerless.

**Congregation:** God's weakness is stronger than our strength; God's foolishness is wiser than our wisdom.

**One voice:** God calls the hopeless, the lonely, the lost.

**Congregation:** God's tenderness chooses us in spite of our needs. God's righteousness saves us in spite of our fears.

**One voice:** God calls each of us to the grace of the cross.

**Congregation:** God is the source of our life. Alleluia!

## Invocation
### (MICAH)

Source of all hope and holiness,
we gather this morning to be church.
Bless those who are absent, but not from our hearts.
Bless those who are distant, but not from your love.
Bless each of us here that we may
kindle justice in our spirits,
draw kindness from souls' wells,
and walk humbly in the path of God. Amen.

## Time of Reconciliation
### (PSALMS)
### *Call to Confession*

The psalmist asks, "Who can abide in God's tent? Who can dwell on God's holy hill?" We all know the answers to those questions and yet we fall short. Let us confess our sins.

### *Confession*

God, we come to you with our honesty—
we try to do what is right,
but sometimes it is easier to bend our values.
We try to speak heart's truth,
but sometimes a small lie is more convenient.
We try to avoid gossip and slander,
but we find ourselves discussing our neighbors.
We try to value people more than money,
but sometimes our choices are based on selfish needs.
Gracious God, forgive us our exceptions.
Strengthen us for the tempting "sometimes,"
that we may walk blameless
in your eyes and in our own. Amen.

### Assurance of Grace

God's holy hill is steep. The grace of forgiveness offers self-understanding and a chance to try again. Praise God.

## PRAYER BEYOND THE CHURCH

### *Prayer with People in Recovery*

#### (MICAH, 1 CORINTHIANS)

We who are in recovery have wearied you, God of grace.
We have entered into years of controversy—
we have argued and pleaded and bargained and cheated—
    you and ourselves.
You sent us prophets—
people who told us the truth,
people who offered us a way out of addiction,
    there-but-for-the-grace way out.
But we didn't listen.
We made wild extravagant gestures—
we burned an offering of promises instead.
Ten thousand rivers of oil were nothing to what we would do,
    if only you would leave us alone!
We were so smart and so broken,
And, yes, we confess that we didn't just damage ourselves.
We would have given our firstborn children
for a drink or a line, chocolate, or a bet.
We were that crazy.
And, of course, we did sacrifice our children.
They will never be the same as those
who grow up without an addicted parent.
We cannot hide from that in recovery.
We only pray their pain may someday become gift,
And give you thanks for recovery,
the simple miracle of recovery,
justice living with all our past and all our present,
kind caring for others who need the help we need,
and a humble walk—one day at a time.

God of the wounded gospel, God of holy-crazy mercy,
we praise you that you receive us, the addicted—
alcoholics and drug addicts, overeaters,
gamblers, and sex and love addicts—
the vulnerable, the weak, the low,
    the despised of the world.
We who are willing to admit we are powerless,
we who are considered least in the world,
we who have to lean on your higher power
    as the source of life.
We are the ones filled with good news.
There is forgiveness!
There is new life!
Christ has chosen the junkie and the drunk,
for we are the ones not afraid to cry,
not afraid to share the love we have received.
The cross? We know both what it's like to hold the hammer
    and feel the nails.
But you, cross-foolish God, humble-walking God,
have all the serenity, all the courage, all the wisdom
    we will ever need.
Amen.

The preceding materials use some of the lectionary readings from the Fourth Sunday after
Epiphany, Year A.

# Searching and Waiting for the Revelation

## (ISAIAH 40:21–31; PSALM 147:1–11, 20C; MARK 1:29–39)

❖ ✂ ❖

## PRAYER OF THE HEART
### (MARK)

*"When they found him, they said to him, 'Everyone is searching for you.'"*
*(Mark 1:37)*

Gentle Savior,
I have been searching for you—
for your healing,
for your good news,
for your casting out
of all those things
that feel to me like demons.

I have wandered in
the sundown of my hope,
and the fevers of
my too-much working.
I have gathered
those I love

and stood at the door,
eager for a personal miracle
that would prove
you love me.

But finally I find you
only in the deserted place,
the place of prayer
where no one else can come
but me,
and I cannot hide.
All my searching
turns around—
you have found me.

## BIBLE STUDY
### Creative Encounter with the Text for a Small Group
#### Wings, Sneakers, and Boots
##### (ISAIAH)

Create a centerpiece with a pair of hiking boots, several pair of sneakers (high-tops, running shoes, tennis shoes), and a wings-symbol (perhaps a kite). Have a stack of construction paper cutouts of wings, sneakers, and boots. Suggest that every human life has times of soaring with joy and success, trudging in grief, pain, loss, and running along a regular course of daily events. In each of these phases, God's support is present in a different way. Ask the participants to identify in which phase they are currently living, choose a cutout, and write a prayer from that place of soaring, trudging, or running. Share the prayers.

## Suggested Questions for Discussion or Personal Reflection
### (ISAIAH 40:21–31)

What reminds you of God's majesty?

When have you felt hidden from God?

When have you felt God to be unjust?

How do you renew your strength?

Is your hope in God like the wings of eagles?

### (PSALM 147:1–11, 20C)

How does God heal the brokenhearted?

When you look at natural beauty, what are your reflections about God?

What does "fearing God" mean to you?

### (MARK 1:29–39)

What was Simon's mother-in-law's response after her fever was gone?

What was Simon's response to seeing Jesus heal people?

What is the nature of response Jesus seeks in those who experience healing power?

Do you seek prayer when you have been exhausted by busy-ness?

## RESOURCES FOR CONGREGATIONAL WORSHIP
## Call to Worship
### (PSALM 147)

Come, flock of voices, sing!
Come and sound your praises to our God!
Come, mount the wings of exaltation!
Come, fledgling choir, and fly!

Have you no loss that God's hand restored?
Have you no break that God's hand repaired?
Have you no strife that God's hand repealed?
Have you no life that God's hand redeemed?

Then lift your voice and sing!
A song of praise—
sweet music of the sphere:
Our God of Life still lives!

# Invocation

Gentle God, you give the stars names,
you feed fledgling ravens when they cry,
  you heal the brokenhearted,
  and you listen to us.
  We come to find your love
  not with horse-strength
  or runner-speed,
  but with our wounds
  and namelessness
  and need for a song.  Amen.

## Time of Reconciliation
(ISAIAH 40)

### *Call to Confession*

We have tried to live our lives alone, not waiting for God's renewal.
Let us confess that we are tired and failing.

### *Confession*

Creator God,
 we push ourselves into exhaustion with petty tasks;
 we offer one another faint-hearted relationships;
 we run after so many good things
  that we run out of energy;
 we depend on our own capacities
  of youth or competence,
  planning or understanding.
Mother-Eagle God, slide your wing under our stumbling,
give us your hand on our weary walk,
forgive us our foolish pride and our self-wasting.
Amen.

### *Assurance of Grace*

God does not faint or grow weary. God's forgiveness is so powerful it could
kill us and so tender it can give us birth.

# Prayer beyond the Church

*Prayer in Grief*

(PSALMS)

*Who Made These Stars?*

Holy One,
Are you the Star-Maker?
Are you the One beyond
the orbs of light you
fling haphazard
to the night?
Are you the One who calls
each orb to task
and tames their errant flight?
Are you the One
who made
these
stars
content?

No Perfect One could know
the dropped-down
iron hand
of fate!
No Perfect One could feel
the blood-chill breakless fear
of falling
out of sight!
Come forth, you Holy One,
before I pass the edge of sound
scream out, if only to my back!
Do not refuse your own
less-equal self
a name.

The preceding materials use some of the lectionary readings from the fifth Sunday after Epiphany, Year B.

# *Called into Revelation*

## (ISAIAH 6:1–13; I CORINTHIANS 15:1–11; LUKE 5:1–11)

❖ ✄ ❖

### PRAYER OF THE HEART
#### (LUKE)

*"Then Jesus said to Simon, 'Do not be afraid, from now on you will be catching people.'"(Luke 5:10b)*

Life-changing God,
you who walk with us before you call us—
willingly we crowd around you to listen to your word,
eagerly we press too close to you,
    wading out to be taught, to be healed,
hungrily we seek to understand you—
    your mission and your presence.

Feed us, Savior, we have worked hard all week long
    and caught nothing to change us.

Speak to us on the shore,
plainly, in images familiar to our daily work.
Help us in our lives and our relationships;
    with the fears and the frailty and the fatigue.
Mend our nets of understanding,
    for they are all torn.

But what is this rowing that you ask us to do—
    to put out into deep waters
    and let down our nets again?
What would you have us catch?
Something that we cannot bring in
    without community, without friends.

Gentle One, leave us—you ask too much of ordinary lives.

But if you say so
and you are not afraid for us
and take us where we need not be afraid—
and bring us back—

caught at last in your life-changing net
at last ready to finish the work of your hands—
the boat-borrowing, net-sewing,
soul-fishing work of your hands.

Then we will leave the ordinary—
we will leave everything ordinary and safe—
we will leave into your calling,
your changing, your grace.  Amen.

## Prayer of the Heart
### (ISAIAH, LUKE, I CORINTHIANS)
*"And I said, 'Here I am, send me!'" (Isaiah 6:8b)*

Burn my lips with a fire which ends pain,
so that I may taste my own words once again.
Net a miracle out of my all-night failure,
so that I am strong enough to leave
the small boats of my past.
Blind my senses,
so that I may begin to see with
my hands and my heart.

Call me to prophesy words I do not understand
and which may not be understood.
Call me to fish with gospel-nets
strong enough to catch even those who flee.
Call me to share the Resurrection
in all its beauty and fearfulness—
the most timely and untimely
blessing of all.

Kneeling in the sanctuary—
here I am, send me.
Working on the seashore—
here I am, send me.
Coursing down the crossroads—
here I am, send me.

# BIBLE STUDY
## Creative Encounter with the Text for a Small Group
### *Picture of God*
#### (ISAIAH)

Cover several tables with brown or white table paper. As people come in, have them find a place and "draw God." Have available crayons and markers as well as glue, glitter, and multicolored ribbon. Participants should spread out, but no one should be at a table alone. After ten minutes, walk around asking people to describe what they drew; then hang the paper on the wall. Make clear that this time we have not used separate sheets of paper because the complete picture is what has been drawn together.

## Suggested Questions for Discussion or Personal Reflection
### (ISAIAH 6:1–8 [9–11])

What did God look like when you were called?

Why is guilt associated with unclean lips?

What is it about speech that needs to be burned holy?

Do we need to volunteer into God's call—"Here I am, send me"—before we know its content?

What has your most powerful experience of God led you to do?

### (I CORINTHIANS 15:1–11)

What do you pass on "as of first importance"? From whom have you received it?

How has Christ appeared to you?

### (LUKE 5:1–11)

When has God "used your boat" to reach someone else?

When have you, with no knowledgeable participation, been the means for someone to be in touch with God?

How hard is it to "let down your nets" one more time—to seek for grace or abundance in your life when experience has been "all-night" negative?

Have you ever been afraid because of a blessing?

Are you willing to leave everything for God?

Are you willing to leave everything to help other people be found by God?

## RESOURCES FOR CONGREGATIONAL WORSHIP
### Call to Worship
#### (ISAIAH, LUKE, I CORINTHIANS)

**One voice:** Let us come to the sanctuary of prophets and angels—

**Congregation:** We share sacred time and holy song.

**One voice:** Let us come to the gospel story of healing and call —

**Congregation:** We share our gifts and promises for living.

**One voice:** Let us come to the gospel affirmation that Christ died for our sins in accordance with the Scriptures, and was buried, and was raised on the third day and appeared.

**Congregation:** Christ is alive! We share Resurrection grace and life after life! Christ appeared for us!

## Invocation

### (LUKE)

Itinerant God, who wanders onto our seashore and uses our boats to reach others, we have let down our nets all week and have drawn them up empty. We come to the dawn of this day weary of even trying. Make miracle in our lives in this hour of worship, that we may hear your call to be fishers of all humanity. Amen.

## Time of Reconciliation

### (ISAIAH)

### *Call to Confession*

The subtlest of all sins are the sins of human speech. Let us confess them now.

### *Confession*

Holy, holy, holy God,
I am a person of unclean lips—
    I have said cruel words,
    and have left unsaid kind ones.
I dwell among a people of unclean lips—
    there are bigoted words about
    race, tradition, age, gender, orientation;
    there are gossip and slander,
    political deceit, false advertising,
    corporate manipulation, religious hypocrisy.

Holy, holy, holy God,
purify my words and send me, angel-driven,
with your message for my world. Amen.

### *Assurance of Grace*

God removes our guilt and heals the burn of its damage in our lives.

## Prayer beyond the Church

### *Prayer with Clergy*

#### (ISAIAH, LUKE, 1 CORINTHIANS)

O holy God of hosts, we have been called—

We have been called by smoking seraphs with wild wings,
and we knew how vulnerable and guilty we were,

and our burned mouths whispered words of willingness
and accepted words of hurting-confusing prophecy.

Gentle seashore Savior, we have been called—

We have been boat-used, fish-surprised, and netted-in,
and again we knew ourselves vulnerable and guilty,
so you led us to a place of not-afraid
from which we were able to leave everything.

Road-hovering Resurrection Riddle, we have been called—

we have been called in the tradition of witnesses
and with the particularity of our own encounter.
Again, in the grace of your choosing us,
our unworthiness was met and known and
given a meaning
which itself became part
of our good news.

Call us again—re-call us,
for we have scrawled years of clergy-graffiti
across the surface of our ministry.

We have felt superior to our parishioners.
We have mocked some,
hated and feared others.
We have been cold and uncaring,
numbed and insensitive.
Sometimes we have not wanted them
to turn and be healed.

We have failed to go to the hospital,
and someone has died;
we have failed to go to the nursing home,
and someone has been lonely;
we have failed to make time for a word . . .
ignored a look of pain,
passed by a reaching hand.

We have broken confidence.
We have forgotten to pray promised prayers.
We have treated colleagues shamefully
because of insecurity or pride.
We have said shallow words in funeral homes;
we have taken sides in committees;
we have not suggested change

because of the work involved;
we have preached cheap, flashy sermons—
starving for praise—
and we have been angry
at your Easter children
for their unfamiliar faces.

Some of us have committed sexual and
ethical and financial violence and
we have been caught and not-caught.
All of us have walked the borderline of wrong desire
and cast quick stones to disassociate ourselves
from the sins we most fear.

We have been lonely for you and
have run away from you like hell.
We have been angry at you, and
have grown more pious in our platitudes.
We have become experts at you, and
have not acknowledged the immaturity
of our faith to someone who could pastor us.

Holy, netting, risen One—
we return to our vulnerability and our guilt and our knees
because we remember how forgiveness begins.
Send us a live coal of purification and
a message so difficult
that we falter again.
Make us put out to the deep waters of
silence and meditation and
let down our nets for the love we need
so that we can be fishers of others.
Encounter us in such a journey that we know
we are lost and unfit and amazingly graced.

Holy, netting, risen One—
re-call each of us to these words—
   "I am the least of the apostles,
   but by the grace of God
   I am what I am." Amen.

The preceding materials use some of the lectionary readings from the Fifth Sunday after
Epiphany, Year C.

# Carried into Revelation

(ISAIAH 43:18–25; 2 CORINTHIANS 1:18–22; MARK 2:1–12)

❖ ✄ ❖

## PRAYER OF THE HEART

### (MARK)

*"I say to you, stand up, take your mat and go to your home." (Mark 2:11)*

Healing God, forgiving God—
I do not know what I most need.
I only know that when I am brought
into your presence,
I will be both healed
and forgiven.
There are so many close to you,
who know how to pray,
who listen well,
ministers and deacons,
the popular and successful,
the wise and kind.
In a crowd of witnesses
I cannot reach you
through the saints.

I do not want to be carried.
I know my friends love me,
but their care
makes me feel trapped

in my own immobility.
It is terrible disequilibrium
to trust others, and I will
owe them so much.
I feel the words of release
from the illness of guilt,
and the guilty illness—
from the date rape and the incest,
the anorexia and the addiction,
these body-stiff heartbreaks.

Healing God, forgiving God—
you are glad they brought me,
I can see it in your face
and I am glad
I was carried here—
lifted up and lowered down—
to hear you call me child
and send me home.

## BIBLE STUDY

### Creative Encounter with the Text for a Small Group

#### Option: Asking the Questions

##### (2 CORINTHIANS)

Have each participant take five minutes to write five questions about his or her personal relationship with God to which the answer is "yes." Next, each one should frame one question about his or her personal relationship with God to which the answer is currently "no." Take that question and rewrite it so that the answer could be "yes." Finally, write a prayer based on these reflections.

## Option: Carrying the Person with Paralysis
### (MARK)

(This activity is particularly good with a youth group.) Using a camp bed or stretcher, have each member of the group experience being carried once around the room by others. Several people may not want to be carried but only to be "carriers." Some may say they are too heavy or too tall. Others may have a hard time lying still even for a short time. All should be encouraged to experience the sensation both of being carried and of carrying, even if they are unable to reflect on it verbally.

## Suggested Questions for Discussion or Personal Reflection
### (ISAIAH 43:18–25)

What are your "desert" experiences?

What could be a new way in your life? What is one new beginning that you seek?

What are "new things" God may be doing with the church/the secular realm?

Can you forget your sins if God does?

### (2 CORINTHIANS 1:18–22)

In Christ God always answers "yes." What are the questions?

What does having the Spirit of God in our hearts feel like?

How do we work together to increase one another's faith?

What is mutuality in Christian leadership?

### (MARK 2:1–12)

Who "brought" you to Christ? What efforts were involved for this person/these people?

What has paralyzed you in your life so that you could not seek your own healing?

How do you imagine the paralyzed man felt when he was being lowered through the roof?

What is the relationship between sin and healing?

Why do people become angry when someone receives forgiveness?

## RESOURCES FOR CONGREGATIONAL WORSHIP
## Call to Worship
### (2 CORINTHIANS)

**One voice:** God is faithful; in God is not "yes and no," but always "yes."
**Congregation:** Amen! Let us say "yes" to God.
**One voice:** God's promises find their "yes" in Christ Jesus.
**Congregation:** Amen! Let us say "yes" to God.
**One voice:** Christ seals our hearts with the spirit of blessing.
**Congregation:** Amen! Let us say, "yes" to God.

# Invocation

God of blessings,
we come thirsty for you,
lonely for you,
hoping for you.
Give us rivers in the wilderness-places of our hearts,
tenderness for memories of sadness,
strength for the possibility of new beginning.
Choose us this day, gentle God,
and we shall be chosen.
Form our hearts to your love and
spring forth in us an amazing future.
Amen.

*3-21-10*

53

*Carried into
Revelation*
✢

# Time of Reconciliation
(ISAIAH)

## Call to Confession
Let us name the wilderness.

## Confession

We remember the desert of our heart
   where our emotions were parched and dried.
We remember our prayerless times
   when we said meaningful words to no one.
We remember the weary emptiness
   that burdened us because we gave nothing.

*3-21-10*

O God, do not remember our sins,
   but remember your love for us. Amen.

## Assurance of Grace
God does not remember the former things.
God makes a way in the wilderness—a new way.
God lets us drink at springs of forgiveness.

# Prayer beyond the Church
## Prayer with People in Helping Professions
### (MARK)

We are the rooftop people—
we are pastoral counselors and social workers,
psychiatrists and spiritual directors,
we are twelve-step sponsors, parole officers,
therapists of many disciplines.

We are the rooftop people—
with faith in our faces.

We find the paralyzed one—
the one who cannot come to forgiveness
or inner healing, who is immobile with the past,
and we gather others to help us carry him
to help us carry her, to the healing place.

We are the rooftop people—
strong with the skill of perceiving pain,
of asking questions,
of listening to memories.
We all carry an inflexible person
on a mat woven of words and trust.

We come to the place of healing,
and it is too crowded, and we knew it would be.
There are too many emotionally broken,
spiritually wounded in our world.
How can one patient, client, friend
get through the press of people
in clinics, schedules, meetings?
God, you are there and we could reach you
because we are agile and mobile,
but this person, still with pleading eyes,
prone with pain and locked joints
could never "excuse," shift, dodge,
shove to the center of anything.

We are the rooftop people—
we look for another way in.

We climb to a new perspective point
and begin to dig up the roof mud
where God dwells.
We try other methods, we take risks,
we answer late-night phone calls,
we refuse late-night phone calls,
we ask others' opinions.
and then the roof is gone,
and the opening for the heart,
for the spirit, for the psyche-soul
is only big enough for one.

We are the rooftop people—
we participate in healing
by having a rope long enough for someone
to go away from us without falling.

We see what happens from a distance.
God forgives; God cures.
No one understands why it doesn't matter
which comes first, but we do.
There are two parts to every healing—
and the second one always means
picking up your mat to walk away.

We are the rooftop people—
we watch our mats be carried away.
We do not need to hear "good-bye."
We retrieve the rope of our energies
and breathe freely.

Of course, we also hear anger—
some people don't want others
to have a chance for health,
but would rather label them—
addict, crazy, victim, manic, ex-con,
neurotic, welfare mother—
and would like us
to give up on them, too.

We will not do that.

We are the rooftop people—
we are pastoral counselors and social workers,
psychiatrists and spiritual directors,
we are twelve-step sponsors, parole officers,
therapists of many disciplines.
And all that matters, gentle Healer,
is that you look into our faces,
and smile thanks for our faith,
and we hurry through the crowd ready
to weave another mat,
to lift another frozen child of God,
to scramble wildly in roof mud,
to lower away till rope burns our hands.

And your love at a distance is
all the joy we ever need to know.

The preceding materials use some of the lectionary readings from the Seventh Sunday after
Epiphany, Year B.

# Making a Sabbath-Shaped Space
# for Revelation

## (DEUTERONOMY 5:12–15; 2 CORINTHIANS 4:5–12; MARK 2:23–3:6)

❖ ✣ ❖

### PRAYER OF THE HEART
#### (DEUTERONOMY, MARK)

*"Observe the sabbath day and keep it holy, as . . . God commanded you."*
*(Deuteronomy 5:12)*

Breathe a Sabbath in me, God,
that I may embrace creation—
black tree silhouette against crimson dusk,
winter-white stars, cold and bright,
hard frost, first crocus
March soil-stirrings of animals who rest.

Lead me into a Sabbath, God,
that I may experience your law.
Hold me, still me, fold my restless hands.
Guide me to the holiness of not-doing.
Let me walk strictly in quiet pacings
of the obedience where joy begins.

Lend me a Sabbath bounty, God,
that I may squander it away.
Open me to ease the burdens of others
and offer gentle laughter
to the weary and the worriers,
and even those who bind themselves.

Walk with me a Sabbath that is mine, God,
that I may choose healing.
Feed me the sacred bread I need to grow.
Soothe the withered limbs, the twisted soul.
Teach me to take responsibility
to define all of my days.

Bury me in a Sabbath, chosen-lonely God,
that I may understand forsaken
and hear only silence in my prayer.
Bury me in your borrowed tomb
and let me descend a private hell,
that tomorrow I may wake to resurrection.

# Bible Study

## Creative Encounter with the Text for a Small Group

### Option: Sabbath Time
#### (DEUTERONOMY, MARK)

Have the participants pretend they are each wearing a walking heart monitor and must record their activities. They should list everything they did the day before the class. Have them put a heart beside activities that give them joy, an X by things they wish they did not have to do, and a check by those things that are real necessities. Some items may be marked in more than one way. They should also note what other things are included on the list. Have each participant share his or her list with one other person.

### Option: Sabbath Place—Guided Meditation
#### (DEUTERONOMY, MARK)

With soft music, guide the participants into a reverie about a favorite vacation spot. Begin by having them become aware of their breathing and of the different parts of their bodies, then slowly verbally lead them to a place where they have rested—the colors of that place, the smells and feelings, the sounds. Take at least ten minutes there so that each person can be fully present in the place he or she has chosen. Gently lead them back to the group. Wait patiently for any sharing that might emerge.

## Suggested Questions for Discussion or Personal Reflection
### (DEUTERONOMY 5:12–16)

How do we *observe* a day (really look at it)?

What have been some holy days in your life? Why?

How do we set about to make a day holy?

Why does the commandment specify Sabbath rest for slaves?

Discuss the contemporary issue of service workers being compelled to work on Sundays/Saturdays and holidays?

Do you keep a Sabbath regularly—once every seven days? What do you not do and what do you do on your Sabbath?

What treasure do we have in "clay jars"? our talents in a lackluster job? our hopes when we seem to be too old? our spirit in an infirm body? the possibility of soul-sharing in a preestablished relationship?

How do you understand the church as a clay jar holding the knowledge of the glory of God?

In what particular ways have you experienced Jesus' death in your body?

How does the experience of death or loss in the midst of our lives lead to blessing?

(MARK 2:23–3:6)

When do "good" laws become abusive?

Why was the Sabbath made for us? How does it bless us?

Why are people angry when someone is healed?

Is healing always appropriate/always good? Should healing take place whenever and wherever it can?

What is withered in you that needs to be healed?

## RESOURCES FOR CONGREGATIONAL WORSHIP
### Call to Worship
#### (DEUTERONOMY, MARK)

**One voice:** Sabbath is our time—it was made for us!

**Congregation:** We rejoice in its rest, its prayer, and its peace.

**One voice:** Sabbath is also a time of healing—healing is never forbidden.

**Congregation:** We bring our withered hands, our bleeding wombs, our tomb-shrieking demons, our bent spines. We are invited to come with all that hurts us.

**One voice:** Remember the Sabbath and keep it holy.

**Congregation:** We offer holy bread to one another. We share compassion, justice, and law-bursting love.

### Invocation
#### (DEUTERONOMY, MARK)

We have come to Sabbath, God.
Feed us with your bread of consecration;
breathe in us the Spirit's wind;
kindle flame in the tinder of our gospel;
shelter us in the hollow of your hand.
Abide with us—
that we may touch the human in you
and the holy in ourselves, and
so be filled with grace for this day
and the week that is to come. Amen.

# Time of Reconciliation

## (2 CORINTHIANS)

## Call to Confession

We come to confession; we break open the shells of our lives in the presence of God's love.

## Confession

Potter-God, with the clay of our lives on your fingers—
We confess that the treasure of your love for all people
    is held in the earthen jar of our lack of compassion.
We confess that the treasure of your justice
    is held in the earthen jar of our avoidance of issues.
We confess that the treasure of your peace
    is held in the earthen jar of our restless conflict.
We confess that the treasure of your gospel
    is held in the earthen jar of our church.
Forgive, restore, and sculpt us to your will.
Do not shatter us, but rather mold us to a shape
    in which we can be pourers of grace for others.  Amen.

## Assurance of Grace

God's hands are on us for mercy. The treasure of God's forgiveness is held in the chalice of our faith.

# PRAYER BEYOND THE CHURCH

## Prayer with Juveniles in the Criminal Justice System

### (MARK)

God, help us recognize the Sabbath in the sentence.

Once there were some young men
in a detention center and the
counselor assigned to them
broke the rules—
he brought in trashy novels
to encourage two boys who were illiterate to read.
he used public money to take two others
to a Broadway show.
and he softened all the restrictions
on basketball and lights out.
When they fired him, he said,
"rehabilitation was made for these boys,
not these boys for rehabilitation."

God, help us recognize the Sabbath in the sentence.

> Once there was a young woman in a halfway house
> whose heart was withered away.
> She'd worn out the counselors
> by acting out in group time,
> not taking her meds, and scrawling
> obscenities in lipstick on her wall.
> She never said, "thank you," and
> she took other girls' clothes.
> The case worker who finally reached her
> had ignored other responsibilities,
> and gave the withered girl
> some special favors.
> When they fired her, she said,
> "Is this a place to do good or harm?
> If there is a life to save, shouldn't
> I save it?"

God, help us recognize the Sabbath in the sentence.

Gentle One, God of creation and Sinai, God of grain fields and synagogues,
Let us feel with those who are sentenced to an involuntary Sabbath
from normal life in hopes of their new creation.
Let us remember that what is lawful is not the laws but the life they support—
> and there is no bread so holy,
> no time so special,
> no punishment so deserved,
> no money so sacred,
> no heart so withered or hardened—
there is nothing that should prevent God's children
from stretching out their hope into the healing of their lives. Amen.

The preceding materials use some of the lectionary readings from the Ninth Sunday after
Epiphany, Year B.

# In the Place of Shining

## (EXODUS 24:12–18; MATTHEW 17:1–9)

## PRAYER OF THE HEART
### (MATTHEW)

*"But Jesus came and touched them, saying, 'Get up and do not be afraid.'"*
*(Matthew 17:7)*

Luminous God,
your gift of light
is so hard to hold
in hands of flesh,
and I approach it
with shadows clinging—
scars unhealed,
pain unceasing,
guilt consuming,
fear corroding,
shame demeaning.

Shine grace upon my face;
and into my heart—
so that I may take
the sure-step trail
up which Christ leads me
there to share at last
the light of God.

Yet, even there you have
something else in mind.
Luminous God,
you bid me see
Christ's inner nature posed
revealing all the life
that's real.

This path is not to end
where once I thought—
in my share of light made real,
enshrined and safe
from scar and pain,
from fear and guilt.
It ends in Christ,
who is the light
where life is flesh,
who is the life,
where light is shared.

## BIBLE STUDY
### Creative Encounter with the Text for a Small Group
#### *Transfiguring the Daily*
##### (MATTHEW)

Share an experience of transfiguration. Light a candle and pass it around the circle. Let each person describe an experience from the past week that was holy. Some of these experiences may appear to be very ordinary. Also, remember that holiness and happiness are not the same. Give the participants ample time to think about the week. Someone may feel the need to share something from another time. Welcome that story, but redirect the group to finding holiness in the past week rather than telling the most amazing story. After each person's sharing, invite the rest of the group to respond, "God's holiness transfigures our daily lives." Close the gathering with a simple service of Holy Communion.

## Suggested Questions for Discussion or Personal Reflection
### (EXODUS 24:12–18)

We sometimes experience a feeling that people whom we love are "going into a cloud" where we cannot follow (a spouse going into surgery, a child going to kindergarten or college, an elderly friend or relative slipping into some form of dementia). Share an experience like this. How did you feel?

When have you had a solitary encounter with God?

Describe the appearance of the glory of God.

### (MATTHEW 17:1–9)

When have you seen a person with a radiant face? What was the occasion?

What visions of God have you had?

What needs to be transfigured or transformed in your life?

Peter misunderstood how to respond to the Transfiguration. When have you wanted to set up a shrine around a holy experience rather than taking what you learned from it back to the ordinary?

How do you feel when you leave a transfiguring experience?

## RESOURCES FOR CONGREGATIONAL WORSHIP
## Call to Worship
### (EXODUS)

**One voice:** God who waits on the mountain of holiness—
**Congregation:** Our God calls us.
**One voice:** Our God who shines in cloud and fire—
**Congregation:** Our God stirs us.
**One voice:** Our God who is honored for honesty, love, justice—
**Congregation:** Our God offers us guidance.
**One voice:** Our God who abides in compassion and forgiveness—
**Congregation:** Our God receives us into the heights of worship, so that we may return to our covenant with life.

## Invocation

O Glorious God,
we are a people who love the light of your face.
We come again this morning to experience your radiance.
Look upon us with the glow of your life-healing countenance
and shine us into wholeness.

We bring into your radiant love
the lives of our loved ones, our families, our friends,
even those from whom we are estranged.
Embolden us to shine in their lives with your radiant light.
Amen.

## Time of Reconciliation

(MATTHEW)

### Call to Confession

The luminous God shines in our places of shadow. Let us confess our sins.

### Confession

O Transfiguring God,
we are a people who fear the light of your face.
We offer only reasoned hopes and measured faith,
we build a shrine of isolation around your justice,
we serve the spirit of timidity that shades
your possibilities for ourselves and others.
Turn us around to see your light
transfiguring us into bold new images of your face. Amen.

### Assurance of Grace

One of Christ's most amazing miracles is letting us see ourselves—and see ourselves forgiven.

## PRAYER BEYOND THE CHURCH

### Prayer for the Intensive Care Unit

(EXODUS, MATTHEW)

We enter cloud
and bright revealing light—
we are at once in mystery
and the most vivid
watching of color—
the dazzle of rough white sheets,

the green jaggings
of heart and breath,
the silver jewelry of the room
surrounding the lumpy flesh
with arms bruised a rainbow,
thin red discharge, and

64

*Epiphany*

the urine bag
measuring yellow,
this lumpy flesh
of many human hues,
hurting with the drip and
suture of hope.

We enter cloud
and bright revealing light,
and it is like a mountain
none of the ones we love
expected to climb—
by ambulance
from the accident, or
gurney from the
operating theater,
slumped in the office,
at the restaurant,
over the kitchen table
by heart attack or
stroke-struck—
half-face a cartoon
and words and thoughts
like a thousand-piece puzzle
with no edges.

On this mountain walk the
lawgivers of medicine
and the prophets
of diagnosis, and
we try to shrine them
and shelter ourselves
with desperate
mistaken worship.
Overcome by fear,
we sit on the burgundy
upholstery of
special waiting rooms,
stare at watercolors meant
to be peaceful,

and listen (over the purr
of the television,
the jangle of the phone
from the nurses' station,
and the muted conversations
of other anxious families)
for the voice of God—
and the truth
that some will die here
and some will live
and go to another hospital room,
a room where flowers
are allowed, food
can be complained about,
and children come.

Some will die here
and some will live—
but all will find the Beloved.
We tell no one about this vision
before the Resurrection
makes us sure that
in cloud and coma,
in fire, flatline,
and fluttering breath,
in words of love
and prayers,
and in the gentle hands
of those whose work
is intensive
caring—

Christ is present—not as a miracle
of intervention,
but as the transfiguration
of every lumpy
human body
with its pain and flesh
by holiness
and light.

The preceding materials use some of the lectionary readings from the Last Sunday after
Epiphany, Transfiguration Sunday, Year A.

# Lent

# Empty in the Wilderness

## (PSALM 32; MATTHEW 4:1–11)

### PRAYER OF THE HEART
#### (PSALMS)

*"Happy are those whose transgression is forgiven, whose sin is covered."*

*(Psalm 32:1)*

Forgiving God—
I praise you for the covering of my sin
in soft folds of your garment of love.
I praise you for not accounting to me my iniquity,
nor letting me reckon my value by sin-lists.
I praise you for your hand heavy on me
with gentle urging to draw me out of the toxic silence
that was wasting my very body with guilt.

Forgiving God—
Empty me of my self-sufficient ways and hopes
and pour into me your spirit of repentance.
Create within me the unquenchable desire to forgive
even as I have been forgiven by you.
Lead me to the depths of my heart,
where I can ponder the nature of your holy love
and the unbelievable happiness
of freedom from sin.

Forgiving God—
Teach me the simplicity of confession
and the peace of forgiveness as a way
of living among others.
Bridle me against the stubborn unwillingness
to listen to your guidance.
And help me always choose a posture
of prayer, reconciliation, and trust
in my relationship with others and
my joyful response to you.

# BIBLE STUDY
## Creative Encounter with the Text for a Small Group
### *Stone Soup*
#### (MATTHEW)

Put out salsa, dips, peanut butter, and jam on a tray surrounded only by stones. After the initial laughter, invite the participants to each choose a stone and put it in the center of their paper. Write around the stone all the things each one is "hungry" for in his or her life. Which hungers can be satisfied now, and which ones will need to wait? Put the food away so it is not wasted, but do not eat it during this session. Participants may want to reflect on that choice.

## Suggested Questions for Discussion or Personal Reflection
### (PSALM 32)

How does silent guilt impact our bodies?

How is God a hiding place in time of trouble?

What is confession? What happens in you?

What is the feeling of being forgiven by someone else? by yourself? by God? Describe the happiness of forgiveness.

### (MATTHEW 4:1–11)

Jesus was alone in the wilderness—and yet the scripture speaks about the Spirit, the devil, and the angels. Who comes to you when you are alone?

When should we not turn stones into bread? When are we supposed to keep the stones?

What hungers should not be satisfied?

How is Scripture used demonically?

When have you tested God by doing something self-destructive, and daring God to love you?

How desirable is power? What will you do for professional, relational, personal power?

Have you ever sought power in an unholy way?

What tempts you most?

## RESOURCES FOR CONGREGATIONAL WORSHIP
## Call to Worship

**One voice:** Welcome to the Lenten season. We remember Jesus' journey from Jordan to the wilderness.

**Congregation:** There are places of wilderness and temptation in our lives.

**One voice:** We remember Nazareth and Capernaum—the healings and the parables, storm-stilling, and an abundance of loaves.

**Congregation:** We still need stories and a gentle touch. We long for peace in tumult and nourishment for deep hunger.

**One voice:** We remember the final days in Jerusalem—the garden and the cross and the tomb.

**Congregation:** As we walk the path of these forty days, may the light of their meaning guide the steps of our faith.

## Invocation
### (MATTHEW)

Gentle God, we thank you for this Lenten hour of worship.
Deepen our prayer.
Teach us to understand ourselves,
    to be reconciled with one another and
    to love you with profound joy.
Lead us into such simplicity of faith and honesty of spirit
that, as individual Christians and as a congregation,
we may be strengthened in temptation
and renewed in grace. Amen.

## Time of Reconciliation
### (MATTHEW)
### *Call to Confession*

Let us walk together in an intimate geography of stones and pinnacles.

### *Confession*

Gracious God, we confess that we have deep aching hungers
    and sometimes we can hear nothing but their clamor.
We confess that we risk our well-being and flirt
    with self-destruction, hoping
    that we will be safe and loved.
We confess that we long for power—
    self-control in our own lives,
    dominance in our relationships—
    and we are willing to give too much for this power.
We have been tempted, and we have sinned.
Breathe in the silence of our guilt the whisper of repentance
    that we may receive forgiveness. Amen.

### *Assurance of Grace*

God's grace is given, not grasped. Because we are forgiven, we need not be empty, nor vulnerable, nor powerless ever again.

# PRAYER BEYOND THE CHURCH
## *Prayer with Political Leaders*
### (MATTHEW)

Gracious God, we are tempted to promise,
bread, bread, bread,
in whatever form is longed for,
when we know that there are only—
stones, stones, stones.
It isn't just the desire to win votes
or even just to please the public.
Deep in us we want abundance for people—
easy miracle-like abundance would be preferred.
We do not trust the people enough to tell them
about the necessity for chewing stones.

Bread would feed them and would make us loved—
so any means to bread is appropriate.

Mighty God, we are tempted into risk.
We'll send a few troops here and a few there.
We will say that you protect them
and not your people on the other side,
and then we will comfort the mothers
of those who die.
There will be such excitement—
for there is no excitement like aggression—
the danger, the community-feeling,
the marching, and the prayers.
Everybody really prays for the angels
when we plummet into war.

And we can quote Scripture easily to prove
you are in war a faithful God.

Gentle, crucified God, we are tempted
to worship someone else—
a poll-powerful God, a proven-effective-leader God,
a God who-gives-a-sign-when-asked God,
a God-communicator who awes the Pilates.
Yes, we could handle whole realms of power—
not for bad things, not for ourselves,

but because we could use power for good.
God, empower us for justice—
or we just might find someone who will—
empower us as peacemakers,
empower us to serve the poor,
empower us to save the nation, the state, the city,
empower us, empower us, empower us—

No.

Unpower us, O God, to become servants.
Keep us honest, open to the best ideas
of any political party, willing to compromise
and commit public-image suicide, if necessary.
Lead us by your Spirit sometimes to a lonely place.
Feed us by the angels, strengthen us
against the obvious demons
and against the subtle temptings of
both the evil and the benevolent.

God of David and Esther,
God of the King of the Jews,
you see our hearts, cleanse them.
You know our minds, keep them discerning.
You tend us soul and prickling flesh.
Keep us healthy in body and spirit,
that we may bring honor to this
complicated and difficult profession,
offering justice in our decisions,
humility in our opinions,
compassion for those in need,
and respect for all the people
we seek to serve. Amen.

The preceding materials use some of the lectionary readings for the First Sunday in Lent, Year A.

# Spring Ember Days

"Oh, that I knew where I might find [God], that I might come even to [God's] dwelling." (Job 23:3)

# Night Blessings

(GENESIS 12:1–4A; PSALM 121; JOHN 3:1–17)

❖ ✂ ❖

## PRAYER OF THE HEART

### (GENESIS, JOHN)

*"In you shall all the families of the earth be blessed." (Genesis 12:4b)*

You come in the night to me
calling me out to be a
blessing—telling me
my family will be
star-flung and
shore-sand many.
You come in the night to me
and change my name
and ask me to go
away from familiar,
from home,
to be a blessing for you,
a word, a voice
of God-stroking
for strangers,
and other wanderers
who find in me—
a name and
blessing.

I come in the night to you
a dark-walking prayer,
terrified of giving
life to myself—
life so bloody and
naked and new.
I come in the night to you,
with my questions
and my logic and my
fear of the wind,
and you meet me with
world-embracing love,
world-relishing love,
and you open your womb,
your warm, soft,
deep-red womb
to hold and expel me—
a birth and
blessing.

## PRAYER OF THE HEART

### (GENESIS, PSALMS)

*"[God] will keep your going out and your coming in from this time forth
and forevermore." (Psalm 121:8)*

O God of pilgrims of all the ages,
you called Sarah and Abraham to travel unknown ways,
encouraged Rebekah to leave her home for a life of promise,
and herded Jacob and his family into confrontation with Esau.
Indeed, your chosen people walked to Egypt and back.

Thank you for the care and vigilance you've shown as guide and guardian.

Praise you for being a God who ventures losing certainty
    in exchange for gaining trust.
Bless you for meeting trust with steadfast love and mercy.
Forgive me, when I doubt the wisdom of your restless heart.

O God, who yourself became a pilgrim,
lift up my eyes to see you in human form.
Stir me to recognize you and believe that you journey still with me.
Inspire me, Holy Spirit, to ask for your help in revealing
    that the pilgrim Christ walks on
    through me in all that I say and do
    when I express God's love.

# BIBLE STUDY

## Creative Encounter with the Text for a Small Group

### *Born Again*
### (JOHN)

Take a wide, shallow, beautiful bowl and fill it with water. Let each participant blow across the surface and watch the ripples of his or her breath. Remain in silence for a few moments. Ask everyone to share a birth story.

## Suggested Questions for Discussion or Personal Reflection
### (GENESIS 12:1–4A)

When have you been afraid of going forth to a strange place?
What is it to "be" a blessing?—not "give" a blessing or "offer" a blessing—but "be" in such a way that others are blessed?
If you thought God would bless those you bless and curse those you curse, how would that change your speech?

### (PSALM 121)

What earth-places, natural places, do you gaze upon for strength?
Have you ever thought God was asleep?
When do you feel God closest: in daytime activities or nighttime hours?
In what ways do you experience God's help?

### (JOHN 3:1–17)

When have you tried to hide your relationship to God?
What is second birth?
Are you afraid to trust yourself to something as ill-defined and windlike as the Spirit?
If God loves the world so much, can you love it? Or do you deal in world-condemnation?

# Resources for Congregational Worship

## Call to Worship

### (PSALMS)

**One voice:** We lift up our eyes to the hills seeking help.
**Congregation:** The God of mountains, the World-carver, is our help.
**One voice:** God, our Pathmaker, does not let us stumble into wrong ways.
**Congregation:** God, our Watcher, does not sleep in times of trial.
**One voice:** God, our Father, shields us from scorching sun by day.
**Congregation:** God, our Mother, sits by our bedsides in moonlight hours.
**One voice:** Strong God keeps us from evil, from doing and suffering evil.
**Congregation:** Gentle God sustains our life day by ordinary day.
**One voice:** Holy God keeps our going out and our coming in—
**Congregation:** In this time of worship and all the days of our lives.

## Invocation

### (GENESIS, PSALMS)

Holy One, be among us—
>    day and night,
>        hill and valley,
>            sure-path and stumbling.
Bless us that we may be blessers.
Guide us that we may venture forth with courage.
Keep us as we come in to worship
>    and as we go out to serve you in the world. Amen.

## Time of Reconciliation

### (JOHN)

### *Call to Confession*

Let us admit the unborn and the dispirited in us.

### *Confession*

Gentle Teacher—
>    We are embarrassed by seeking you.
>    We are confused by the language of "born again."
>    We are terrified of vulnerability
>        and suspicious of anything aimless.
>    We don't believe you really love the world.
Holy Teacher, we would shape a more polished confession,
>    if you didn't question all our preconceptions,
>        and still accept our willingness to come to you. Amen.

*Assurance of Grace*

God is not an explanation.
God is a wind-blower;
God is a birth-giver—
and we can be born.

## PRAYER BEYOND THE CHURCH
*Prayer with Women Who Must Begin Again* *
(JOHN)

I am too late to be born again—
I have given birth to children and dreams,
and the eggs are old
and my time is past.
I have given birth to myself—
I have counted all the answers
for my life and sought no more questions.

I am closer to dying than childhood.
I am wrinkled and not supple.
I do not easily curl into you
into the darkness
of the swirling sack
of all your sacred fluids,
into the cavern of your love for the world.

How can I be swallowed by the
lonely-blows-where-it-will
place in God—
where I am no longer
respectable or expectable,
where I cannot retire on my honor,
nor fold my hands in comfortable wisdom,
where there is uncertainty every morning
and I lie down to sleep in doubt,
where there are no answers, no condemnation,
and no one else's opinion matters?
And yet there in the throbbing-warm place in God
I am not left helpless, fetal-unfinished

*Women who return to the work force after a divorce or the death of a spouse, or who are forced or called into a second career.

to float in peace—
but must be thrust raw-newborn,
vulnerable, wet and cold,
wailing for the loss of your heartbeat
and my sweet old age,
into new beginning and
crazy, painful, holy life.

The preceding materials use some of the lectionary readings for the Second Sunday in Lent, Year A.

# Mud Blessings

(1 SAMUEL 16:1–13; JOHN 9:1–41)

❖ ✖ ❖

## PRAYER OF THE HEART

(1 SAMUEL, JOHN)

*"[God] said, 'Rise and anoint him [David] for this is the one.'"*
*(1 Samuel 16:12b)*

Come, Spirit of blessing, anoint me
with your oil of promise.
Do not look on my appearance,
but look on my heart, and
choose me into courage for
the future you have planned.

Come, Savior of grace, heal me
with your mud of spit and dailiness.
Open my eyes that I may no longer
approach life as a beggar,
but publicly claim my release
without fear.

Let your oil drip down upon
my hair, my face, my shoulders,
my arms, and my fingers—
sweet and warm and
beauty-smelling like
sunset, flowers, and sea.
Slick in me a spirit of dancing
and playing and joy.
Soften me; scent me;
let my tears be mixed with
the perfume of you, as I cry,
"I am chosen."

Let your mud be cool and dark
on my wounds—finding the
lifelong bitterness, the
fractures of childhood, the
vulnerability of youth, and the
cherished damage that
has become my identity.
Bandage my pain
with your caring, then
send me to wash the past.
Do not protect me from
challenges to my new self,
but seek me out to confirm
my hesitant faith.

Come, gentle God, with
your gifts of mud and oil.
Touch me;
pour on me a holy glistening;
love me till I bathe to peace,
then choose me to tell
your wonderful, dangerous
good news.

# BIBLE STUDY

## Creative Encounter with the Text for a Small Group
### *Mud and Oil*
#### (1 SAMUEL, JOHN)

After discussing the scripture passages and the questions, gather around several bowls of mud and sweet-scented oil. Let everyone put their fingers in both substances and play. Ask some open-ended questions: How do we feel about mud and oil after these passages? What do we want to do with them—touch ourselves, our hands, our eyes, our heads, with one or the other? touch someone else? Does one or the other bother us?

Play with words and fingers long enough to decide together on a common ritual and prayer to close the time together. Share the worship that has emerged from being touched by these scriptures. Provide some wet towels!

## Suggested Questions for Discussion or Personal Reflection
### (1 SAMUEL 16:1–13)

Do you know what it is like to grieve over a relationship that is finished, even when God is calling you into a new one? (Remember: Saul was not dead.)

Do you know what it is like to carry away the oil of your affection and yet fear retaliation from the person in your old relationship? (Remember: Saul was powerful.)

Do you know what it is like to stand there with the oil of your affection and no idea on whom you are to pour it? (Remember: David wasn't even present.)

What does it feel like not to be chosen?

What does it feel like to be chosen?

What is the relationship between oil and spirit?

### (JOHN 9:1–41)

Where do you find traces (or more) of the belief that people cause their own misfortunes?

Does being healed make you unrecognizable by your former associates and friends?

What is God's mud?

What fears divide parents and children?

What kind of healing is driven out?

How do blindness and sin play off each other in this passage?

How do judgment and healing play off each other in this passage?

# RESOURCES FOR CONGREGATIONAL WORSHIP
## Call to Worship
### (1 SAMUEL, JOHN)

**One voice:** This is the day which God has made.
**Congregation:** Let us rejoice and be glad in it.
**One voice:** Any day is holy; all time is given by God and precious.
**Congregation:** But we set aside the Sabbath for the resting of the Holy Spirit.
**One voice:** Let us open our minds and hearts to an anointing of blessing.
**Congregation:** Let us open our souls and bodies to a healing of grace.

## Invocation
### (JOHN)

Gracious God, accept our morning prayers of praise:
for this dawn's rosy-fingered light,
for this day's blue-green planet spin,
for this dance circling back from night,
and the awe-filled miracle of grace,
this rising of the sun.

Accept our morning prayer of petition for light to shine:
on this day's hidden wound,
on this day's tight-shouldered stress,
on this day's anguish and despair,
and on all your many children
living under the sun. Amen.

## Time of Reconciliation
### (JOHN)

### *Call to Confession*

Dwelling in the story of Jesus' healing of a person born blind, let us acknowledge our intolerance and our misperceptions.

### *Confession*

Healer of blind hearts,
we confess that we see what we want to see and
do not understand what we do not want to understand,
and we become defensive when our definitions are challenged.
We drive out those whose healing makes us uncomfortable—
addicts, the mentally ill, people with prison records.

We refuse to allow our children or our parents to change
from situations of dependence.
We condemn what is not familiar—
we label other faiths—cults,
we disparage acupuncture or hypnosis,
aromatherapy or herbal medicine.
We imply that people are responsible for their misfortunes—
people who are unemployed, people with disabilities,
children in foster care.
Judge us into repentance, touch us with humbling,
and send us to wash in your pool of blessing. Amen.

## *Assurance of Grace*

Christ came into the world to judge and heal. We who confess our sins to God
are fully forgiven.

# PRAYER BEYOND THE CHURCH
### *Prayer with People with Disabilities*
(JOHN)

We are people with disabilities—
our eyes do not see for us;
our ears do not hear for us;
our tongues do not speak for us;
our limbs do not move as others' do.
Some of us have holes in our hearts;
others take insulin or Lithium or Prozac;
some of us can name a disease and
others can remember an accident.
Some of us have a lifetime of being in this body,
others are learning difficult new skills.
Some of us are bitter;
some of us are grateful;
some of us are angry with God.

We are people with abilities—
we speak with our fingers,
we read with our hands,
we paint with our feet,
we spin the wheels of wheelchairs,
we have dogs more trustworthy than people.

We understand the pain of others;
we listen to stories longer;
we are skilled at waiting;
we are inventive in overcoming barriers—indeed,
we are wildly creative in everyday living.

We love God,
but we are wary of the Scriptures,
bruised by generations of preachers,
and hesitant of the community called church
which so often defines healing and
leaves us on the outside of it.

Precious God, God who embraces
our rage and our pain,
our pride and our joy,
in your magnificent love,
we are claiming this story,
radically, fiercely claiming—
wheelchair and white cane,
ASL, bells-on-stoplight and curb-cuts,
feeding tubes and braces—
claiming this story as our passionate prayer.

We praise you, God, that you declare us
guilt-free of our disabilities and
we thank you that we are chosen
for your works to be revealed in us—
as *we* name those works.

We rejoice, God, that we encounter you,
and we need never beg again.

We love you, God, for breaking the Sabbath—
for touching us against the law.

We acknowledge to you, God,
that our disabilities tear our families apart
and that our parents and spouses and friends
often do not want us to be independent.

We cry out to you, God, that many people
secretly believe we have caused our disability—
we are responsible,
we are embarrassing,
we are perhaps contagious.

We pause in wonder, God,
that Jesus comes to those driven out,
those kept out, those who are not welcome.
Jesus comes down the stairs and
outside the too-narrow door to invite us into faith.

We affirm, O God, that Jesus reverses all expectations—
blind is not sin—those who say they see are sinners;
deaf is not sin—those who say they hear are sinners;
mentally ill and lame and mute and dyslexic are not sin—
only people who judge others by
body-law, barrier and begging
have locked themselves inside
the one truly inaccessible place,
which is no sanctuary.

We are people with disabilities and abilities,
hurt and laughter,
memory and hope.
We know healing beyond all definitions.
We know the glory of God that looks like mud.
We are not afraid to be driven out and
we are not afraid to believe.

Amen.

The preceding materials use some of the lectionary readings for the Fourth Sunday in Lent,
Year A.

# Twisting Blessings

## (NUMBERS 21:4–9; PSALM 107:1–3, 17–22; JOHN 5:1–8)

## PRAYER OF THE HEART

### (NUMBERS, JOHN)

*"Do you want to be made well?" (John 5:6b)*

Lift before my eyes
in brazen display
the source of my death
that has twisted out of me
and out of my generation
and turned to kill us.

In the courage of my looking
is my healing.

Help me grip the mat
that I lie upon
rather than be deluded
by the mirage of someday
being assisted to an
angel-agitated pool.

In my wanting wellness
is my healing.

## BIBLE STUDY

### Creative Encounter with the Text for a Small Group

#### *Hanging Serpents*
##### (NUMBERS)

Identify the things that poison our lives: attitudes, like anger and jealousy; interpersonal events, like incest or deception; systematic violence, like racism, toxic waste, corporate greed. Write the words on thin strips of paper and twist them around a pole, or write them on a large hanging "serpent" form. Go around the circle and voice them aloud. Discuss why naming them and "hanging" them in a visible way aids healing.

### Suggested Questions for Discussion or Personal Reflection
#### (NUMBERS 21:4–9)

When have you become impatient with the wandering in your life?
What makes you angry at God?
What is the connection between anger and poison?
When does looking at the thing that has damaged you bring healing? Why is this true?

What are some serpents that have not been hung up to be seen, exposed, acknowledged (e.g., clergy sexual abuse, political corruption, "fixed" athletic competition, etc.)?

(PSALM 107:1–3, 17–22)

How do we make ourselves sick by sinfulness?
How does God heal?
In what ways do you trust medical science?
How do we turn to God?

(JOHN 5:1–8)

What does it feel like to be in a place where many people with illnesses and infirmities gather? What is the feeling of a hospital?
What does companionship have to do with healing?
How does it feel (honestly) to let go of an old illness?
What is the difference between getting in the water for which everyone is longing and being healed?
What questions does God ask that you answer with excuses?

## Resources for Congregational Worship
### Call to Worship
(PSALMS)

**One voice:** Give thanks to God who is good.
**Congregation:** God's steadfast love endures forever.
**One voice:** We cry to God in our trouble.
**Congregation:** God redeems us and heals our lives.
**One voice:** From East and West, God gathers the wanderers.
**Congregation:** From North and South, God saves us from distress.
**One voice:** Let us tell of God's works with songs of joy.
**Congregation:** God's steadfast love endures forever.

*5-10-09*

### Invocation
(NUMBERS, JOHN)

> Gracious God, we turn our restless spirits to your healing
> and encounter your peace and passion
> in the gathering places of our society.
> Bless us in this sanctuary where we seek
> the intimacy of worship, and bless us
> throughout the wanderings of our daily lives.
> Amen.

*5-10-9*

# Time of Reconciliation

## Call to Confession

Let us confess to God in chosen words and in self-searching silences.

## Confession

I confess that I poison myself with anger,
    bitterness,
        regret,
I confess that I cripple myself with excuses,
    complaining,
        procrastination.
I repent.
I am ready to look at the most painful parts of my life and live.
I am ready to answer the hardest question—
    the question of whether I am willing to change.
Show me.
Ask me.
Forgive me. Amen.

88
*Lent*

## Assurance of Grace
### (JOHN 3:14–17)

As Moses lifted up the serpent in the wilderness
so Jesus Christ has been lifted up
in precious abandoned love for the world.

We are not condemned—
we are saved.

# PRAYER BEYOND THE CHURCH
### *Prayer with Journalists*
### (NUMBERS)

God, we set the serpents on their poles—
the slick, ugly, killing serpents.
We name the poisons in society—
and society is not grateful.

We search out the scandals of politicians,
and haunt organized criminals with
respectable jobs.
We expose corporate greed
and find the toxic waste sites.
We column the injustices

of foster care and welfare,
of courts and churches.
We photograph the poor
with rats in their homes,
and children dying where
smart bombs have fallen.
We scalpel the hospitals where
people should not have died,
and do time with convicts who
should not have been beaten.
We publish stories of priests and

pastors,
teachers and police officers
who have betrayed their callings.

In Tehran and Sarajevo,
in Detroit and Boston,
in headline, against deadline—
we report on the world's
twisted things—
and we do not turn back
from the fangs,
and sometimes we die.

God, we are not the news,
we only report the news.

We are not the violence,
we only name it.
We are press and we press—
we ravage reputations,
interfere with investigations,
sensationalize the sinister
with our hands on
the snake-tail of truth.
In newsprint and videotape
we bronze out the coils
of danger and deceit.
Unless we hang them
where all will see—
no one can be healed.

## Prayer with Hospital Chaplains

### (JOHN)

Five porticoes
many invalids
and one deep pool
where sometimes an angel stirs.

We walk the halls
and ask question of
those who come to this
modern-day Bethesda.
We ask about wellness—
and the hopeful ones
answer about treatments—
angioplasty and chemo,
radiation and medication,
surgery and therapy.

We love them all,
and we pray with those
who are going to be
doctored down the steps
to the pool
at the right moment,

and we pray
with those whom we know
will never touch the water,
but still long for magic.

Do you want to be well?
No, I can't put you in
the pool, but
I can tell you about
one who can help
you take your own life,
mat and all,
into your own hands.

Even in the lonely place
with five porticoes,
many invalids,
and one deep pool
where sometimes an angel stirs

there is deep healing.

The preceding materials use the Hebrew Bible and Psalms selection from the Fourth Sunday in Lent, Year B. The gospel reading is found in the lectionary on the Sixth Sunday of Easter, Year C.

# Resuscitating Blessings

(EZEKIEL 37:1–14; PSALM 130; JOHN 11:1–43 (11:44–12:11))

## PRAYER OF THE HEART
### (JOHN)

*"He [Jesus] cried out in a loud voice, 'Lazarus, come out!'" ( John 11:43)*

Life-summoning God,
Keeper of the gate that leads to everlasting life:

The one you love is asleep.
We pray you come without delay,
that this sleep may not end in death
but in your glory
and in the glory of your Child.

Come wake the one you love.
Come draw this sleeper back
from wandering in the life-effacing haze
of lowly self-esteem.
Call out this sleeper's name.

Come wake the one You love.
Come draw this sleeper back
from sinking in the life-suppressing mire
of unforgiven shame.
Call out this sleeper's name.

Come wake the one You love.
Come draw this sleeper back
from floating in the life-suspending state
of emotional self-disgrace.
Call out this sleeper's name.

While there are yet hours in the day,
while sun and earth spin face to face,
while light conspires to shine,

call out this sleeper's name.
Draw forth the one you love
from resting in the grave.

## Bible Study
## Creative Encounter with the Text
### *Acting Out the Story*
#### (JOHN)

Gather in a circle to read this story aloud, with volunteers taking the different parts: Jesus, Thomas, another disciple, Martha, Mary, a mourner, stone-movers, and unbinders. Carefully choose a person willing to play Lazarus. Wrap this person from head to foot in toilet paper. Cover the face, and bind the arms to the sides and the legs together. Seat this person in a chair in another room. Close the door. The group that remains reads the story slowly. Act out the raising of Lazarus, having the stone-movers open the door and the unbinders very slowly and carefully unwrap the tissue, beginning with the legs and ending at the face. Let all participants share their feelings about the experience.

## Suggested Questions for Discussion or Personal Reflection
#### (EZEKIEL 37:1–14)

How does it feel when God asks you to prophesy to something that you can see is dead? hopeless? foolish?

What dries out bones? How is hope lost?

How are the Church—and our churches—like dry scattered bones? List the ways.

This is a story about stages in resurrection: bones coming together and then breath coming into the body. The second could not happen without the first, but the first could happen without the second. Reflect on times in your life which are represented by these images.

#### (PSALM 130)

Alcoholics Anonymous talks about the need to "hit bottom" (and that everyone's bottom is different). Do we need to reach the depths before we cry to God?

What does forgiveness feel like, look like? What color is it? What is its sound?

What are the occasions when we "watch for the morning?" How does that feel? Why does waiting for God feel like that?

#### (JOHN 11:1–12:11)

Why did Jesus delay going to Lazarus? How do you think Martha and Mary felt about it?

Is it all right to be angry with God when someone we love dies?

Why does Jesus weep in this story? Why does Jesus weep in our day?
From what kinds of death does Jesus raise us?
How do we participate in the unbinding of others?

## Resources for Congregational Worship
### Call to Worship
#### (EZEKIEL)

**One voice:** Sometimes we experience life as disconnected bones. We rattle around
our lives without hope.

**Congregation:** But God promises open graves and vibrant spirits.

**One voice:** Sometimes we are cut off from one another and all our sources of
joy are dried up.

**Congregation:** But God promises we can be a community, filled with understanding and care.

**One voice:** We gather in this place to hear God's Word and feel God's Spirit.

**Congregation:** God knits together our brittle lives and limbers up our dry
souls, so that we not only live, but dance!

### Invocation
#### (EZEKIEL)

O gentle God, you are the only source of healing and resurrection. When we
are lifeless, like dead bones in a desert valley, you splint us together and cover us
with the flesh of your grace. Then you entice, catapult, trick, pry, lure, love,
blackmail, and jump-start us out of the graves of our meaninglessness. Amen.

### Time of Reconciliation
#### (PSALMS)

### *Call to Confession*

Come to the depths—
  the depths of your memory,
  the depths of your fear,
  the depths of your shame,
  the depths of your emptiness.
Come to the place where your foot touches hope,
  and you can begin to cry.

### *Confession*

Holy God, we confess that we watch for the morning rather than waiting for you.
  We expect a string of new days when we do not need
    to remember the past.
We trust the cycle of life, the rhythm of things as they are—
  failing to disrupt injustices around us.

We speak glib daybreak phrases that have cut off
　　the halting expression of another's pain.
We waste today and count on tomorrow—
　　avoiding the needs of our spirits and our bodies.
And sometimes we lay sleepless and too angry to pray
　　or be reconciled with a friend.
Gentle God, lead us to a repentance that is a timelessly open waiting for you.
　　Amen.

### Assurance of Grace

There is forgiveness with God as beautiful
as the color of a lonely dawn
when we have forgotten to be
desperately awake.

## PRAYER BEYOND THE CHURCH

### *Prayer in a Shelter from Domestic Violence*
### *(Spoken by two women: first voice,* JOHN; *second voice,* EZEKIEL)

*First voice:*

I have been battered dead—
hurt to death, wrapped in silence,
sealed in a tomb of
accusation and guilt.
I have been battered dead
too long—
my life smells dead
even to me.
I hear the love of sisters
from a muffled distance,
but it does not keep me alive.

*Second voice:*

I have been scattered dead—
my hope dried up,
the bones of my life
just so much valley-rubbish—
some education here,
self-respect there,
a job I used to love,
high school sports,
best friend I don't want
to call on the phone,
a photograph of myself

not wearing sunglasses,
and my children . . .
even if I pulled these
fragments of who I used to be
into some reasonable skeleton,
it wouldn't be enough—
you need breath
to walk away.

*First voice:*

I am alive now because
somebody got angry at God,
and prayed my pain so hard
Jesus cried.
I am alive now because
somebody moved the stones
of house and reputation,
of family, courts, and police,
and somebody
unwrapped me from
fears and insecurities.
I am alive now because,
when God called "come forth,"
somebody came forth—
somebody like me.

*Second voice:*
God, you bone-rattler,
you fibula-stirrer,
you dancer in the skull,
you digit-counter, knuckle-collector
until I have enough fingers
to throw away the key.
God, you wind-whistler,
you breath-breather,
lung-pumper, till I am
full of one great shout,
"enough!"

I am alive now because
you opened my grave,
splinted the splinters
of my life,
spirited my spirit,
and gusted wild prophecy
in somebody powerless—
somebody like me.

The preceding materials use some of the lectionary readings for the Fifth Sunday in Lent, Year A.

# Hosanna Blessings

(ISAIAH 50:4–9A; PSALM 118:1–2, 19–29; LUKE 19:28–44)

❖ ✄ ❖

## PRAYER OF THE HEART
### (ISAIAH)

*"The [Sovereign] God has given me the tongue of a teacher, that I may*
*know how to sustain the weary with a word." (Isaiah 50:4a)*

Give me the tongue of a teacher,
a gentle tongue.

Touch my tongue with your fingers,
that I may know how to sustain,

that I may recognize weariness
in tired lines around lonely eyes,
and stroke knotted shoulders,
and breathe into myself
the exhausted sigh,

that I may choose my word well,
not many words, just
one kind word.

Waken in me the ear of a listener
a listener who is taught,
by spring song of morning nesting,
or beggar haunting of seagull,
by the God-full words of strangers
or the easy-to-ignore stammerings
of those I know too well,
even by the memory
I have never spoken
to myself.

Oh, waken in me an ear that listens to
more
even than these—
let me listen not only to bird call,
but to wind under feathers.

Let me listen to root.

Let me listen to shell spiral an
echo of the sea.

Let me listen to the hollowness
where there is unprayed prayer,
and the brightness
where there are voices
in the sky.

Soul mother, open the portals in me—
tongue and ear and spirit.
Open me for wounds and worship,
unweary me
to share your love.

# BIBLE STUDY
## Creative Encounter with the Text for a Small Group
### Option: Crying Stones
#### (LUKE)

Take a pile of stones and a roll of masking tape. Tape words onto the stones, telling what they would cry out—first, long ago in Jerusalem, and then today. Some of the words may praise God and some may lament Christ's death or the abuse of the earth. Make a small mound of the "crying stones" in the center of the class.

### Option: Meeting the Procession
#### (LUKE)

Invite the participants to leave and take a walk for ten minutes. Ask them to visualize, while they are walking outdoors, what it would be like if suddenly the Palm Sunday procession appeared. Would they join in the "Hosannas"? Would they be curious? enthusiastic? bewildered?

Ask them to note what they do see on their walks. Discuss the experience when they return.

## Suggested Questions for Discussion or Personal Reflection
### (ISAIAH 50:4–9A)

How do you have the tongue of a teacher and the wakened ear of a listener?

What words sustain the weary?

When is it (when has it been for you) appropriate to submit to abuse?

When is it (when has it been) appropriate to declare "not guilty" in the face of everyone else?

### (PSALM 118:1–2, 19–29)

"Open to *me* the gates of righteousness"—why is this in first-person singular?

What does a stone that builders reject look like? What did Jesus as a Messiah look like?

Can we, do we, must we rejoice in every day that God makes?

### (LUKE 19:28–44)

What do you let God borrow—just let go because "God needs it"?

Has there been a time when all the miracles of your life have made you burst out in song? When?

What statement was Jesus making by this strange procession?

How do stones and trees, earth and oceans cry out—about holiness, about violence?

# RESOURCES FOR CONGREGATIONAL WORSHIP
## Call to Worship
### (LUKE)

**One voice:** Blessed is the Messiah who comes in humble victory.

**Congregation:** Blessed is the Savior who rides through hope-songs and stone-weeping.

**One voice:** Blessed is the Messiah who entered the dangerous streets of Jerusalem long ago.

**Congregation:** Blessed is the Savior who enters the uncertain terrain of our lives today.

## Invocation
### (PSALMS, LUKE)

Hosanna, save us, you who stand on the threshold
while we fling the cloaks of our praise before you.
Hosanna, save us, Messiah, so misunderstood.
Hosanna, save us and open the gates to us
of hope and prayer and peace. Amen.

## Time of Reconciliation
### (LUKE)

### *Call to Confession*

Let us confess how much we are like the Jerusalem people of long ago.

### *Confession*

Holy and gentle God,
We confess that we want you to meet our expectations
rather than changing our lives to meet yours.
We confess that we are often changeable and self-centered
like the Jerusalem crowd, shouting "Hosanna"
one day and "Crucify" the next.
We confess that we prefer the festivity of Palm Sunday
to the quiet sadness of Holy Week.
Forgive us all our sins and help us take up
our own crosses to follow you. Amen.

4-5-09

### *Assurance of Grace*

When we cry "Hosanna," God enters our lives with forgiveness.

# Prayer beyond the Church
## *Prayer with People in Advertising*
### (LUKE)

After the parade,
love me, God.

After the Hosanna
in the brightest wordy
jingle, sound byte,
save me, God.
After I've organized the donkey
and started the trend
for cloak-spreading,
after I've convinced
even the stones to cry,
after the record-breaking
end-of-season
special
frenzy of "Blessed"
that will turn
to "Barabbas!". . .

After the parade
of my life,
and the sleeping,
the kissing, and the
hand-washing
of an easy world,

take me, God,
to the place of
a morning crowing
for the taste of tears,
and teach me
the things that make
for peace.

The preceding materials use some of the lectionary readings from the Sixth Sunday in Lent, Year C. The Hebrew Bible reading is from the Liturgy of the Passion, and the gospel and psalm are from the Liturgy of the Palms.

# Easter

◈ ✄ ◈

# Setting the Resurrection Free

(ISAIAH 65:17–25; 1 CORINTHIANS 15:19–26; JOHN 20:1–18)

## PRAYER OF THE HEART

### (JOHN)

*"But Mary stood weeping outside the tomb." (John 20:11a)*

Out into the morning mists
I come, alone,
one last time to see you.
I stoop to touch you,
bathe you with my tears again,
wrap you in my gaze of love
for who you were.
But here in the half-light of dawn
the stone is rolled away.
The linen cloths are cast aside.
No body lies within this tomb.

But strange words gently spoken
beckon me beyond my misty view,
"Why are you weeping?"
At first but dimly heard
and, then, a second time,
repeated clearly,
a voice calling me by name.
O God, this is
my life's great healing teacher.

This is the voice I hear—
the same voice I knew,
the face I see—
the same face I loved.
My knees give way,
my heart and hands reach out
to hold the one I knew as good
who died before my eyes.

"Do not cling to me,"
come even stranger words,
and I kneel before a mystery.
Your death was real,
and you are real.
The light now fully dawns
before my eyes that you
have left the tomb behind.
And I, I too, to live with you
must let you die for me
to set my new life free.

## BIBLE STUDY

### Creative Encounter with the Text for a Small Group
#### *Christmas and Easter*
##### (JOHN)

Set up a crèche in the center of the table. Spend some time in quiet reflection or listening to Christmas carols. Use some of the following questions to guide discussion:

Which do you prefer: Christmas or Easter? Why?

Share a vivid Christmas memory and a vivid Easter memory.

What are the themes of each of these holidays? How are they similar? How are they opposite?

The stories of the Nativity and the Resurrection are the least fully developed in the Scripture. Why?

Why do we use physical objects such as Nativity replicas for Christmas and emblems of emptiness (empty tomb, empty cross) for Easter?

## Suggested Questions for Discussion or Personal Reflection
### (ISAIAH 65:17–25)

If you were going to create a new heaven and earth, what would be their characteristics?

What projects (houses, vineyards) would you like to undertake and know that you will be the one to enjoy them?

What things make a long life a good life?

Reflect on the idea of ecological harmony being one of the results of Easter.

How is the salvation of creation parallel to personal salvation?

### (1 CORINTHIANS 15:19–26)

What do you believe happens to personal consciousness after death?

When is death an enemy?

When is death not an enemy?

### (JOHN 20:1–18)

What is the greatest loss you have ever known?

Why is it disturbing when something is not where you buried it?

What people or things do we hold onto that we should let go?

What does the empty tomb of Jesus of Nazareth mean to you?

## RESOURCES FOR CONGREGATIONAL WORSHIP

## Call to Worship
### (ISAIAH, 1 CORINTHIANS)

**Congregation:** Be glad and rejoice forever—

**One voice:** We shall enjoy the work of our hands. Children shall be raised in security, and old people shall live long and with honor. The natural world shall be in harmony, and no more shall there be human weeping or the cry of distress.

**Congregation:** No one will hurt or destroy in all God's holy mountain.

**One voice:** God is creating a new heaven and a new earth.

**Congregation:** God began with one resurrection.

**One voice:** God is putting an end to death.

**Congregation:** God began with one life.

# Invocation

(JOHN)

Radiant God of light and love,
you fill our hearts with joy this day
by raising Christ to new life.
Receive us as we come to find you
even in the places of death.
Send us forth shining with
Christ's Resurrection in our lives. Amen.

# Time of Reconciliation

(JOHN)

## Call to Confession

We are conscious of our enchantment with mortality which keeps us from expecting the Resurrection.

## Confession

O holy God, forgive us our sins.
We cling to those who have died and
are bound by our memories of a perfect past.
We hold tight to our preconceptions about God
and are unwilling to experience the holy in new ways.
We clutch the Easter holiday rather than
letting Resurrection change our lives.
Meet us in the garden of weeping
and forgive us our fears and sins. Amen.

## Assurance of Grace

Christ is risen—and all our guilt and sin are left behind in the tomb.

# PRAYER BEYOND THE CHURCH

*Prayer with Funeral Directors and Those Who Work in Funeral Service*

(JOHN, 1 CORINTHIANS)

We are intimate with the last enemy.
We help people believe in death
and not believe in death.
We make up faces
and set hair and
glue lips so that
ravaging illness can be forgotten.
We offer lovely rooms
for conversation
and hours for condolence
which have a structure
and an end.
We call priests and ministers
to recite the soft old words
of faith so that
people can let go
their clinging to those
they have loved,

and find, through the weeping,
the Gardener of the soul.
We drive long cars
and talk or do not talk.
We carry caskets
or help those who need
to carry them and feel
the weight of death
to turn corners.

People criticize our costs
and smooth words.
We are called insensitive.
Yes, we have jokes and stories
and banter with the clergy
in self-protection.
We must hold so much grieving
slightly away from our hearts,
except sometimes—
when we lay out straight
the child's limbs,
try to mold peace
on the suicide's face,
dress the pregnant mother
to be pretty
for her other children,
caress the thin hair
of our old schoolteacher,
remember laughter
of a neighborhood friend
with prostate cancer.

If we wept for every death,
who would do the caring?
If we wept for every death,
would anyone believe us
when we say (with the
gentle efficiency of
correct obituaries
and guest books,

discreet handling
of divided families,
and all the other details
people entrust to us)
this one must ascend to God
while you go on?

But we can say this just as surely—
if it is for this life only
that you hope—
then listen to those of us
who have held so many cold hands,
lay satin across so many
gray faces,
waited for the cemetery crew
to come from behind the bushes
and lower so many caskets
in the rain,
and banked so many
carnations and roses
on mounds of dirt—
if for this life only
you have hope, then it is
a terrible pity.

We understand, more than anyone,
that only when we drive
the hearse away
and return to the office
to receive
one more phone call
choked with tears,
only when all the living leave,
do stones roll and
angels wrap up grave clothes.
Only on the other side
of all our skill with
bodies and comfort,
does the Resurrection begin.

The preceding materials use some of the lectionary readings for Easter, Year C.

# Doubting and Faithing

(I PETER I :3–9; JOHN 20:19–31)

❖ ⚶ ❖

## PRAYER OF THE HEART
### (JOHN)

*"A week later his disciples were again in the house, and Thomas was with them. Although the doors were shut, Jesus came and stood among them and said, 'Peace be with you.'" (John 20:26)*

Life-raising God, hear me!
Forgive your pray-er's doubt:
not that another's eyes
can't see for me,
not that another's hand
can't touch for me,
but no other one
can know my fear for me.
No other knows the wounds
that keep me bound.
No other's heart recoils
when my will gives in.
No other lies awake at night
haunted by my demons.

Life-raising God, reach out—
this doubtful pray-er asks for all—
and breathe an active soul into this room.
Blow peace into me,
shape me by your Spirit's power
to bear the image of your Child.
Recall each one of us to see
our wounds, our fears, our sin
were hung upon his cross.
This new body to be wholly Christ
must bid each member come into the tomb
to die to old self-raising ways,
to die to what we are without—
the breath of Christ's new life within.

Life-raising God,
send me out beyond these doors
to wear your wounded side and hands
as signs of hope to every weary soul.
My body has been pierced by hate and fear
but my wounds are being healed by love.
My body lives to sow the seeds of life
in waiting hearts that seeing me,
believe the risen Christ is real.

## Bible Study

### Creative Encounter with the Text for a Small Group
*God's Breath*
(JOHN)

This story of the receiving of the Holy Spirit is gentler than the fire, wind, and tongues of the Pentecost story. It is presented with an image that is intrusive in contemporary terms. We avoid one another's breath and pay a great deal of attention to breath hygiene. Yet "spirit" and "breath" are expressed by the same word in both Hebrew and Greek.

Discuss the concepts of spirit and breath. Spend some time in breathing exercises and meditating on how breath enters and leaves the body. Then go around in the circle and ask each person to breathe on the person to his or her right, saying, "Receive the Holy Spirit." Discuss whether the experience felt comfortable or not.

### Suggested Questions for Discussion or Personal Reflection
(JOHN 20:19–31)

When have you chosen to forgive or "retain" the sins of another person?
What is doubt?
What proof of God do you need? When have you needed proof of God?
Which stories in the Bible (if any) cause you to believe?

(I PETER 1:3–9)

How do you experience your faith as an inheritance?
Describe an experience when your faith was tested.
What things do you believe in that you have not personally experienced?
What things do you love that you have not personally experienced?

# RESOURCES FOR CONGREGATIONAL WORSHIP
## Call to Worship

**One voice:** Come to the risen Christ—you who are fallen.

**Congregation:** We come with our sins, our fears, our doubts, and our sorrows.

**One voice:** Come to the risen Christ—you who are wounded.

**Congregation:** We come with our emptiness, our mourning, our anger, our loneliness.

**One voice:** Come to the risen Christ—you who are rejoicing.

**Congregation:** We come with our hopes, our faith, our pride, and our joy.

**One voice:** All are welcome in the Alleluia!

**Congregation:** All are risen in God's great Amen!

## Invocation
### (JOHN, I PETER)

Life-raising God, we pause to give you thanks for the witnesses you send us. We come to know anew your gift of faith to us through their eyes which saw you standing with them and through their hands which touched your risen body. Fill us, we pray, with the awesome certainty their senses told them—your risen Child is real. Give us the assurance not of sense, but of faith and imagination, and send us into the world to speak new life to others. Amen.

## Time of Reconciliation
### (JOHN)
### *Call to Confession*

We come to the Resurrection like Mary and Peter and Thomas—frantic and shameful and doubting. Let us speak our feelings.

### *Confession*

Risen Savior, we stand in the light of the Resurrection, and we cast our own shadows.

We do not expect our lives to be changed by your presence.

We focus on discouragement and disappointment,
rather than sharing good news.

We let our doubts overwhelm us, rather than helping us grow.

Accept the burden of our faithlessness,
lighten our spirits with your forgiveness

and let us rise into your peace. Amen.

### *Assurance of Grace*

Perhaps John asked Mary and Peter and Thomas, "Can I tell your stories?" And they responded, "Yes, we who were broken are whole."

# Prayer beyond the Church

*Prayer with Scientists*

## (I PETER, JOHN)

The path to believing
travels through doubting,
and understanding
means accepting not knowing,
and testing is the way
to joy—even when
it's hard, long,
and lonely.

The inheritance
of others
is a story of signs
pointing to a reality
which is shadow
and wall-walking
and wonderful.

There are new galaxies
and new elements.
There are possible
particles and species
and cures.
Our faith is search
and research.

If I doubt enough
I can put my finger
inside the hole
in the hand of God.
If I believe enough,
I will be blessed
by what I cannot see
or measure or touch—
the experiment of
the Resurrection,
a hypothesis
for life,
and quantum
holiness.

The preceding materials use some of the lectionary readings for the Second Sunday of Easter, Year A.

# Dawn Christ and Broken Journeys

## (JOHN 21:1–19; ACTS 9:1–20)

### PRAYER OF THE HEART
#### (JOHN)

*"Just after daybreak, Jesus stood on the beach." (John 21:4a)*

I walk the shore
searching for seaglass—
blue and green and white shards
of breaker-smoothed brokenness.

Out of the waves and winds and rocks
you ask me if I love you.

Three times you ask—
three times I remember
how I have fled
and hurt
and denied you,
and cried bitter, bitter tears
for the look without reproach
in your face.

Three times I remember—
three times you ask me
if I love you,
out of the waves and winds and rock.

Searching for me
you walk the shore.

## BIBLE STUDY
### Creative Encounter with the Text for a Small Group
#### *Breakfast with Christ*
##### (JOHN)

The scripture from John provides an opportunity for an informal Eucharist including the eating of fish after the bread and before the passing of the cup. A very simple liturgy, which includes an opportunity for prayers of both thanksgiving and intercession from all participants and a passing of the peace, will draw the group closer and allow them to consider what "having breakfast with Christ" means in their lives. Perhaps passing the bread for a silent prayer of blessing by each participant and lifting the cup so that all can touch and consecrate it will create a sense of sharing. Saying the words, "Christ asks, 'Do you love me?'" when the fish is passed can recall the intensity of Peter's recommitment.

## Suggested Questions for Discussion or Personal Reflection
### (JOHN 21:1–19)

When have you gone back to old ways even after a "resurrection experience"?

"All night fishing—coming up empty" is a repeated life experience. How do you deal with that reality?

Form a mental image of having breakfast—your breakfast—with Jesus. What would you discuss with him?

How is breakfast different from communion?

When has your love been questioned? How does it feel?

When someone else questions your love, how does that mirror your internal voice?

How do we undo our denying of God?

What tending and feeding are asked of us because we love God?

### (ACTS 9:1–20)

Has your faith journey included a conversion story? Tell the story.

Has someone been an Ananias for you—a nervous but willing eye-opener and spirit-giver?

Has God ever asked you to be an Ananias—to offer grace to someone who has hurt your friends? whom you don't like? of whom you are fearful?

How does God get our attention when we are on a path of destruction?

## RESOURCES FOR CONGREGATIONAL WORSHIP
## Call to Worship
### (JOHN)

**One voice:** Come and have breakfast with God. Warm yourself at the charcoal fire of love. Eat fish on the beach with the joy of Resurrection in your heart.

**Congregation:** We come out of the emptiness of night before dawn, out of the loneliness of our sorrows and our guilts. We are so focused on denying in our lives that we cannot see the rising.

**One voice:** Come and respond to love with love. Spread your nets for it. Jump into the deepest place and swim for it. Cry out your pain until you find it in your own words.

## Invocation
### (JOHN)

Gentle God, you know everything, and so you know that we love you. Open that love to be the source of nurture and care for others. Help us to follow you both where we want to go and where we do not want to go. Amen.

# Time of Reconciliation

## *Call to Confession*

To confess our sins is to stop in the path that we have chosen—
   it is to fall down before the brightness of God.

## *Confession*

Risen Christ, we confess that we are breathers of violence.
We are dangerously sure of our rightness and righteousness.
We wield religion as a weapon and seek to bind and subdue
   those who do not believe as we do.
We use verbal, emotional, and spiritual violence
   in our personal relationships.
Risen Christ, shine the terrible light of your truth around us,
   and help us take the hands of those who would
   lead us to grace. Amen.

## *Assurance of Grace*

God's flash of painful self-revelation is the beginning of forgiveness. We repent, and it is a gift. And then God sends us people who lay hands on us for healing and Holy Spirit.

## PRAYER BEYOND THE CHURCH
### *Prayer Acknowledging One's Own Bigotry*

(ACTS)

Road-blocking God,
stop me in the path of destruction
with bright truth
and a ground-kissing,
and a first-time-knowing
that I never saw.

Change me in the hands
of those I would not touch.

Let them heal me
in the courage of their fear
of the racism, sexism,
homophobia, so many
other bigotries—
the breathing violence

of my former hatreds,
which have been beating
and binding you.

Use me, name-changed
and converted;
make the passion
of my persecution
become the passion
of your love
for all of those
outside the boundaries;
send me beyond Damascus,
farther than anyone
not forgiven so much
would be willing to go.

The preceding materials use some of the lectionary readings for the Third Sunday of Easter, Year C.

III

*Dawn Christ and*
*Broken Journeys*
⊰⊱

# Choosing for Easter

(ACTS 9:36–43; REVELATION 7:9–17)

❖ ✄ ❖

## PRAYER OF THE HEART

### (ACTS)

*"When they had washed her, they laid her in a room upstairs." (Acts 9:37b)*

I washed her

little limbs so long and quick
that used to run like a gazelle,
left foot just turning in.
I lay elbow clean against
the rough sheets and
gently touched the ribs
like white lattice
where the flowers of life grew,
when she was
morning glory and roses.

Her hands so still
that worked so hard
and played, too—
gestured whole stories
making a pageant
of her spoken words.
Those sewing hands and
writing hands, those
cooking, earth-planting,

teaching hands, now
little waiting hands.
And then I wept.

And softly fingered things
that once were hers—
the fabric of a dress for dancing
and the shells found
one seashore summer,
the edge of painted dresser,
a square of quilt,
an old photograph
in a pewter frame,
the books she read,
a blue and white bowl,
a silver cross, a ring.

Come to this Joppa, God,
send a healer to
wake her eyes.
pray her alive,
my Tabitha, my friend.

## BIBLE STUDY

### Creative Encounter with the Text for a Small Group

*Going to Heaven*

#### (REVELATION)

Begin with a relaxed "brainstorming" session and list all the imagery of afterlife you know as a group: streets of gold, clouds, harps, the river of life, Saint Peter with a book, a tunnel of light—anything from childhood, your imagination, or television preachers. Draw the focus away from any "damnation images," but honor their reality for people by listing them.

Now spend ten minutes in a group meditation on heaven. Play gentle music in the background, but offer little guidance beyond deep breathing and comfortable posture. Let each participant spend five minutes writing down personal images before being influenced by others. Then share the imagery and reflect on the relationship between the first list and the personal lists.

## Suggested Questions for Discussion or Personal Reflection
### (ACTS 9:36–43)

What will people have to show of your love when you die?
Have you ever wanted to bring some particular person back from death? Why?
What miracle stories do you know which are like this one? remission? a person coming out of a coma?
On what is your faith based?

### (REVELATION 7:9–17)

What is your vision of heaven?
What does "washed in the blood of the Lamb" mean to you?
In what personal way do you wish God would care for you?
What are angels?

## RESOURCES FOR CONGREGATIONAL WORSHIP
## Call to Worship
### (REVELATION)

**One voice:** Let us come before God with our joys and riches.
**Congregation:** God gives us shelter and bounty and blessings.
**One voice:** Let us come before God with our sorrows and fears.
**Congregation:** God wipes every tear from our eyes.
**One voice:** Let us come before God with our doubts and questions.
**Congregation:** God is our Shepherd and guides us to the waters of life.
**One voice:** Let us come before God with our prayer and worship.
**Congregation:** Blessings and glory and wisdom and thanksgiving and honor and power and might be to our God forever and ever. Amen.

## Invocation

Gracious God, we enter the house of prayer and find we are home. We walk in the path of tradition, and the rhythm is our own heartbeat. Welcome us today as we become a community of faith in your Resurrection. Lift our spirits in song, shelter our hearts in prayer, take our hands in offering. May our words and meditations be acceptable in your sight, O God, our Strength and our Redeemer. Amen.

# Time of Reconciliation

(ACTS, REVELATION)

## Call to Confession

In word and silence we confess our sins.

## Confession

Easter has come and yet our lives are not changed.
We accept the power of death in us.
(pause)
We give up on healing and hope for others.
(pause)
We witness many forms of death around us.
(pause)
Roll away the stones from our hearts, that we might
welcome Easter into the center of our lives every day. Amen.

## Assurance of Grace

Salvation belongs to our God, who is seated on the throne, and to the Lamb!
Let us give thanks that we are saved.

# Prayer beyond the Church
## Prayer with Prisoners of Conscience
### (revelation)

We are from every nation,
we are from every language,
robed in the white of death—
washed in our own blood,
washed in our own blood.

Out of the ordeal of cattle prod,
and the ordeal of mutilation,
out of beatings and shocks,
rape and the forced witnessing
of rape, out of false
trials and bright-light
interrogations,
waving palms of innocence,
we come—
victims of cruelty and bizarre
human pleasure.

Such blood-washed children—
only a Lamb-God can understand;
and only a crucified God
are we willing to trust. . . .

We will be sheltered,
who have seen our homes burn.
We will hunger and thirst no more
who have starved and begged
a drink for our child.
The sun will not strike us,
nor will we be struck
and twisted and bruised.
And there will be no scorching
of cigarette burning in our flesh.

For the Lamb will be shepherd
of many slaughtered lambs,
and we will drink deeply
from springs of eternal life,
and God will wipe away
every tear from our eyes.
Yes, God will have to
touch our faces
for a long, long time,
gently smoothing all
the scars and creases—

for we have wept
many tears.

The preceding materials use some of the lectionary readings for the Fourth Sunday of
Easter, Year C.

# House of Stone and Love

(JOHN 14:1–21; ACTS 7:55–60; 1 PETER 2:2–10;
PSALM 31:1–5, 15–16)

❖ ✀ ❖

## PRAYER OF THE HEART
### (JOHN)

*"Lord, we do not know where you are going, so how can
we know the way?" (John 14:5)*

God of many rooms
prepared for those
who place their trust in you
before their journey's done—
where is my heartway home?

Into occasions' simmering pot
where brews the measure of my fear,
I dip my bread and taste
Betrayal's demon enter me—
a poisoned dart quick past
the dozing sentry of my faith
to lodge fast in my disappointed heart.

Bitter steeps the leaves of my despair.
The light I need is lost to me,
departed where I cannot come.
The love I need is thrust from me,
disowned by lips I call my own.

God of many rooms,
I ask for help.
I ask for you to calm
the troubled chambers of my heart
with your gentle knowing
that I'm afraid to trust.

Sweep clear my unmet expectations
of how truth ought to be for me:
a sight I see as proof my trust is safe.

Prepare in me, I pray,
the place where I can free
my deepest fear of being left afraid
to trust again the love I one time knew.
For when I come to trust your love again,
I'll find my heartway home.

## BIBLE STUDY
### Creative Encounter with the Text for a Small Group
*Floor Plan*
#### (JOHN)

Have each participant draw a floor plan of a house in which she or he has been very happy and has known caring and tenderness. This might be a current home, a childhood home, a grandparent's home, or a friend's home. Label rooms and draw in furniture. Take time to describe the homes to one another in loving detail.

Read John 14:1–3 and reflect on God's house, not as a vast labyrinth for many people (or a place that keeps certain people away from one another!) or as an interfaith afterlife, but as a network of beloved homes.

## Suggested Questions for Discussion or Personal Reflection
### (JOHN 14:1–21)

To what place do you go when your heart is troubled?
What kind of a room do you think God prepares for you?
What road markers lead you to God?
How do you recognize the spirit of truth?
How does falling in love with God happen?

### (ACTS 7:55–60)

What is spiritual gazing?
How do you respond to messengers of information that you don't want to hear?
Where have you hurled stones at truth?
Where have you condoned the hurling of stones at truth by not intervening?

### (1 PETER 2:2–10)

Where do you find the milk of spiritual honesty to drink?
Where does your living stone fit in God's spiritual house?
When are you apt to stumble over the cornerstone of your faith?
What is the wonderful light of your life?

### (PSALM 31:1–5, 15–16)

How do you protect your integrity when under attack?
Where do you ask for help in time of trouble?
Why would God help you in your ordeal?
What smile has saved you from distress?

## RESOURCES FOR CONGREGATIONAL WORSHIP
## Call to Worship
### (PSALMS)

**One voice:** O God, You are our refuge in time of need.
**Congregation:** We come, O God with praises on our lips for your power to redeem those who put their trust in you.
**One voice:** O God, let your people not be ashamed for long.
**Congregation:** Be for us a living stone of strength, a solid rock of faith, to save us from the hidden snares of life that now enfold us.
**One voice:** Into your hand we place our spirit's span of days.
**Congregation:** Do not disappoint us our hope; let your face smile upon us, your people of faith, who turn to you for help.

## Invocation

(I PETER)

Into your steadfast hands our spirits pour their cries for strength, O God. Hold the fears we bring to light with gentle kindness. Heed our spoken and unspoken needs that live within our heart. May the milk of your goodness be sweet upon our tongues. Draw us close beside your Child, Christ Jesus, and bid us rest upon Jesus' love for you. Change us to become as Christ is, a living stone, that makes for you a new house—a spiritual house where mercy and steadfast love live in this world. We pray in Jesus' name. Amen.

## Time of Reconciliation

(ACTS)

### *Confession*

Grace-filled God of mercy, throw open your doors. I stand in need. Your light of truth has fallen on my face, and I have turned away. Your word of love has fired my heart, and I have stopped my ears. The stones I throw to keep your Spirit still have hit their mark. I stand outside your gaze of love in every wound I cause. Forgive my sin. Forgive my rush to prove you wrong. Forgive my rage that I live so poorly the life I want to live. Accept my repentance, I pray in Jesus' name. Amen.

### *Assurance of Grace*

Christ Jesus, judge of hands with stones and hearts of flesh, you hear our repentance. You do not hold our sin against us, and you grant us peace that passes all our understanding, so that we know the grace of God and are a forgiven people.

## PRAYER BEYOND THE CHURCH

*Prayer with Hospice Workers*

(JOHN, I PETER)

Gentle God, all the rooms
we enter are holy,
and your dwelling place
is the homes of people
who are building
the spiritual houses
of their own death.

We reach out and touch
the living stones
of the real places
where people have lived lives,
not hospital rooms

with their bright clean
impersonal shining,
but the worn-carpet,
nicked coffee table, and
old black-and-white TV
with pictures of children,
maybe grandchildren,
proudly lined up on top
kind of places.

We bring equipment here—
a hospital bed, a toilet,
a walker, and we set

a schedule of visits,
and we promise—
heart in our mouths
hoping it can be true—
that we can provide the
medication that
will control pain and symptoms
with dignity
until death comes.

We are truly a chosen people,
privileged to share
so many sacred moments—
good-byes woven of
silence or simple words,
families gathered in
unspoken companioning,
forgetting arguments
but remembering love,
and dyings of many kinds—
gentle and beautiful,
angry and remorseful,
unfulfilled or
just far too young. . . .

And when they all turn to us
and whisper,
"How can we know the way?"
we tell them, God,
that you prepared
a kitchen with yellow oilcloth
tablecloth and a basket
of biscuits on it
for a person we knew once,
and a white porch
with a swing, morning glory
and a long-eared dog
another time,
a den full of books, old maps
and chairs soft with memories
of conversations,
and a deck that looked over
the ocean deep blue like
at Hampton Beach,
and a playroom with
storybooks and games
where all the rocking horses
and the velveteen rabbits
were real. . . .

And you will prepare a room
just like this one,
except, it's at home with God.

The preceding materials use the lectionary readings for the Fifth Sunday of Easter, Year A.

# Thirsty for the Spirit

## (PSALM 63:1–8; ACTS 10:44–48; JOHN 7:37–39)

❖ ✣ ❖

## PRAYER OF THE HEART
### (PSALMS)

*"My soul thirsts for you." (Psalm 63:1b)*

I have been in a dry and weary land
where there is no water—
I give you the gift of my great thirst.

I have been filled with emptiness,
seeking you, fainting—
I give you my crazy expectation of your feast.

I have lain awake on my bed,
tossing with broken dreams—
I give you my watching for the shadow of your wings.

The deepest longing,
the naked prayer,
the pause when there is no proof of God,
the lonely wait,
the unblessed day—
I lift before you this magnificent offering,
and my soul clings to you.
Amen.

## BIBLE STUDY

### Creative Encounter with the Text
### *An Experience of Water*
#### (PSALMS, JOHN)

Prepare seeds or seedlings, soil, and paper cups. Plant the seeds in the paper cups, then pass a watering can to one another. Next, pass a bowl of water and towels and wash and dry one another's hands. Finally, fill a communion tray of glasses with water. Offer it to one another, saying, "May you have living water." Discuss the ways in which water fills needs in our lives.

## Suggested Questions for Discussion or Personal Reflection

### (PSALM 63:1–8)

What are the physical aspects of the soul's desire for God? How is this desire "felt"?

Do you think of God differently when you are in the sanctuary from when you are lying on your bed at night?

What is it like to be in the shadow of God's wings?

### (ACTS 10:44–48)

How do you express the gift of the Holy Spirit?

What do you think about speaking in tongues?

How important is baptism to you? Can you tell a baptismal story?

"In what name" were you baptized? Did you know that people were sometimes baptized "in the name of Jesus" rather than with a Trinitarian formula?

### (JOHN 7:37–39)

For what are you thirsty in your life?

What flows out of your heart? Is it something that can be perceived by others? Is it a blessing?

How do you experience the receiving and giving of Spirit in your life?

## RESOURCES FOR CONGREGATIONAL WORSHIP
## Call to Worship

### (PSALMS)

**One voice:** O God, our God, we seek you—our souls thirst for you.

**Congregation:** Dry and weary, we faint for your presence.

**One voice:** We come to the sanctuary to praise you.

**Congregation:** We lift up our hands and call on your name.

**One voice:** Our souls are satisfied in you.

**Congregations:** Our mouths praise you as a rich feast.

**One voice:** We meditate on you in the watches of the night.

**Congregation:** On our beds we remember your constant help.

**One voice:** In the shadow of your wings we sing for joy.

**Congregation:** And our souls cling to the hand of your love.

## Invocation

### (PSALMS)

Thirsty, we come to you. Faint, we lean on you.

Meditating, we dwell in you. Wing-shadowed, we sing to you.

Turn to us in our need with your abundant grace.

Gift us as we worship with a fragrant blessing of Spirit. Amen.

## Time of Reconciliation

*Call to Confession*

Let us remember our baptisms—and confess our sins.

*Confession*

Waterfall God, God of bright sparkling Spirit—
we confess that your word has dried up in our hearts and
that we let ourselves become spiritually thirsty.
We confess that love and hope and peace do not pour out
from us into the lives of friends and strangers.
We confess that we withhold blessings from others
because they don't fit our definitions.
Open the floodgates of your Spirit—
wash our lives with your streams of healing. Amen.

*Assurance of Grace*

Let us remember our baptisms—and trust our forgiveness.

# PRAYER BEYOND THE CHURCH

*Prayer with Christians Facing the Multiplicity of Spirituality*

(ACTS)

We are confused—
by New Age spirituality and crystals,
by goddess-talk and Christa,
by borrowings of Native American traditions
and Zen Buddhism,
by charismatics, faith healers,
and snake-handlers,
by Tai-chi and yoga,
by twelve-step spirituality
and spiritual direction,
by contemplatives and revivalists,
by Christian Scientists and Mormons,
by Jehovah's Witnesses and the
Jesus Seminar.

We can have respectable dialogues with at least
six clearly defined world religions, but
not with these upstart heresies.

But your Holy Spirit doesn't care about orthodoxy.
The Spirit's gift is poured out on those
who don't come to our churches,
who don't sing our hymns,
who don't need committees or
pledge campaigns or even sacraments.

You touch the tongues of all these strangers
and they taste praise; you bless their lives
and they are converted.
Spirituality—it is so unrestrained,
so profligate, so unexpected,
so free of our control.
We can't keep water from them,
when they are flowing with your love.
God, take our hands—bring us close enough
to be splashed.

In the lectionary, Acts 10:44–48 is read on the Sixth Sunday of Easter, Year B; Psalm 63:1–8 is read on the Third Sunday in Lent, Year C; and John 7:37–39 is read on Pentecost, Year A.

# Pentecost

# Day of the Red Spirit

(ACTS 2:1–21; PSALM 104:24–34, 35B, ROMANS 8:22–27)

❖ ✄ ❖

## PRAYER OF THE HEART
### (ACTS)

*"All of them were filled with the Holy Spirit and began to speak in other languages as the Spirit gave them ability." (Acts 2:4)*

O In-dwelling God,
God of the mountains for Abraham;
God of broad places for Isaac;
for Hagar, God of hope and courage;
for Jacob, God of struggle and blessing,
seen face to face;
for Esther and David, a royal God;
for Jonah, a Hunter;
for Joel, the Daycomer
of the blood-red moon
and the radical words of
young women and men.

In your wisdom and loving kindness,
you have shown yourself to be
particularly what each one
longs to find,
and now you speak in a tongue
each one needs to hear.

After Jesus had returned to you,
when all his friends and his mother
gathered in that upper room to pray,
The Spirit touched their tongues
with foreign speech,
or was it just a band of Galilean drunks?

O In-dwelling God,
Aim me to find the Christ
in the man Jesus;
set me to hear the Spirit in jumbled words

and too-familiar Scripture;
then, flame me, wind-fill me
to stumble into
prophesy and power.

## Bible Study
### Creative Encounter with the Text for a Small Group
#### *Wind and Word*
##### (ACTS)

Cover a table with red cloth and give everyone a red prayer shawl. Put angel chimes in the center of the table or suspend wind chimes over a candle so that lighting the candle moves the air and makes a sound. Light the candle(s). Name the powerful imagery of the Spirit: rushing wind, tongues of flame, the descending dove, and the color red. Invite the group to share stories of times when an image or a natural phenomenon gave them a sense of God's presence (seeing a rainbow after someone's death, watching stained glass windows almost come alive—experiences people have and often want to share about God touching their lives through physical reality).

Then pass out newspaper clippings of stories in which the good news is present in the contemporary world. Strive for a variety of experiences—certainly both evangelism and social justice ministry—and a diversity of settings in the global community. Have each participant identify what the Spirit is doing in her or his newspaper story and arrange the articles on the cloth around the candle.

### Suggested Questions for Discussion or Personal Reflection
#### (ACTS 2:1–21)

What do you think the Holy Spirit is?

When have you been filled with unexpected power?

Why is it important that the church begins in many languages?

When have you had the experience that a public speech or a sermon seemed to be suddenly speaking directly to your situation?

#### (PSALM 104:24–35)

How is God's Spirit in all creatures?

Do you relate God to earthquakes and volcanoes? How?

Reflect on this phrase: "God is the play-maker of the whales."

#### (ROMANS 8:22–27)

What is hope?

When have you hoped in something you could not see?

Have you ever prayed in tongues/experienced someone else praying in tongues?

Have you ever been unable to pray but felt that something in you was praying? Describe the experience.

# Resources for Congregational Worship
## Call to Worship
### (ACTS)

**One voice:** We have come to a place of the Holy Spirit.
**Congregation:** In this sanctuary there are healing and hope, wind and fire.
**One voice:** We have come to a community of the Holy Spirit.
**Congregation:** Our sons and daughters are prophets; Alzheimer's patients dream
dreams; Generation X sees visions.
**One voice:** We have come to a time of the Holy Spirit.
**Congregation:** We expect the unexpected.

## Invocation
### (PSALMS)

May our singing be all praise
and our meditations be pleasing,
for we breathe your breath and
are alive with your Spirit.
Do not hide your face from us,
but touch us
like your holy mountains,
so that we tremble and rejoice. Amen.

## Time of Reconciliation
### (ACTS, ROMANS)
### *Call to Confession*

Let us invite the Spirit in so that we can begin to pray.

### *Confession*

We confess that we are more pleased by the grace notes of Christmas and Easter
than the fervent urgency of Pentecost.
We confess that our worst nightmare is sounding drunken or foolish.
We confess that this birthday-church isn't always a party.
We confess that we rarely listen to the speakers of other languages,
and almost never try to learn their words ourselves.
Holy One, we are heart-cut and frightened by the wind.
We repent. Amen.

### *Assurance of Grace*

This is good news—
Spirit . . . in you . . . in me . . .
groans
sighs
too deep for words.
Amen.

# Prayer beyond the Church
## Prayer Outside the Doors of a City Church
### (acts)

Tongues of flame lick up the edges
of the newsstand,
a rush of violent wind
funnels its roar down the tower

and from the sanctuary door strange language
for those gathered into the city—

the couple on the bench, he
with his thatch of white hair,
she with thin sweater and
old-fashioned courtesy, and
the tireless hawker of "Spare Change"
newspaper of the homeless,
within the shelter of his loudness,
the man with the eight-hundred-dollar
suit, too-tight Swiss shoes, and
the hungry-eyed Emerson College girl
with her breast-cancer survey,
the confused couple with Maine plates,
turning up Dartmouth Street
for the fifth time, and
the stylish woman with many laugh wrinkles
around her eyes and her grandson
in a running stroller,
the next-door neighbor to the stone library lions,
who talks to them all the time, and those
who are afraid to meet his old eyes;

and hundreds of others
of all nations, voices, colors, abilities,
sexual orientations and ages,
and, for that matter,
dreams and doubts and fears,
who have nothing at all
in common, but the one hand
upraised to push through the Copley
subway station turnstile gate,
and the possibility of unexpectedly hearing
a word from your gospel

pouring crazy Spirit on their flesh
this Boston nine o'clock morning
of understanding.

The preceding materials use some of the lectionary readings for Pentecost, Year B.

# Summer Ember Days

"Set me on the rock that is higher than I!" (Psalm 61:2b)

# Entering the Long Season

❖ ✀ ❖

## PRAYER OF THE HEART
### (JOHN)

*"When the Spirit of truth comes, he will guide you into all the truth."*

*(John 16:13a)*

Unfolding God—
jagged
granite
souls
you tumble,
breaking in
upon this world
as Word.
Do you come
to make us
cobbled beaches
pummeled smooth
by tidal chargers
wearing down
our edge
to round?
Left to time's
life-grinding
rhythms
even granite
slips
away.

Come and finish
what you started.
Seal your truth
into our body.
Pour your scent

upon our hands.
Rub your spirit
deep down
shining,
splendid spirit fire
shining,
seeping inwards—
shine
our soul.

Come
from the depths
that break upon us—
not a new-set
spinning orb—
loose
the bound up
borrowed grain of
gladness
shared
at birth
before
we fall.

Finish shaping
fullness
in our nature;
perfect

image
moistened
to completion.
not a
hurried pounding
to submission,
but a
slow step
waxing
into
love.

May the tumbled
stone
unfolding,
perfect
shape of God
unknown
be
the ground-down
stillness
rising
lifting up
the face of God.

# BIBLE STUDY
## Creative Encounter with the Text for a Small Group
### *Wisdom's Circle*
#### (PROVERBS)

Place a ring on top of a table in the center of the group—a large ring of metal or rope or ribbon or beads. Using modeling clay, have each person place a foundation under the ring to hold it up. Ask each person to fashion a "playful Wisdom" figure of clay and put her inside the ring. Discuss together what should go in the center of the ring. Using clay and a votive candle, create a center. Tell the story of your "Wisdom": What does she do? How does she make herself known? How does she matter in your life?

## Suggested Questions for Discussion or Personal Reflection
### (PROVERBS 8:1–4, 22–31)

Where does Wisdom speak to you?
When have you heard Wisdom in your own voice?
Where does Wisdom want you to take a stand?

### (PSALM 8)

How comfortable are you with praising God?
What do you ponder when you look at the heavens?
What is your defense against those who vex you?

### (ROMANS 5:1–5)

Are you at peace with God?
Who brings you into the experience of God's grace?
Do you boast about your sufferings?
Have you been deceived by hope?

### (JOHN 16:12–15)

What is the difference between being told what you ought to know and being led to it?
What do you require in order to learn what is true for you?
Where has the Spirit led you to discover truth?
What does the Holy Spirit reveal to you about God?
How is the mystery of your life revealed to you?

# RESOURCES FOR CONGREGATIONAL WORSHIP
## Call to Worship
### (PROVERBS)

**One voice:** Who calls us to this house of prayer?

**Congregation:** We hear an urgent voice crying for our presence.

**One voice:** Where is the sound of this voice lifted up?

**Congregation:** On the peaks of our joys,
   on the pathways of our daily life,
   at the crossroads of our choices,
   this cry reaches out to us.

**One voice:** Who is wanting us to listen?

**Congregation:** Wisdom wants a voice in our life;
   discernment longs to be heard.

**One voice:** How shall we listen?

**Congregation:** With ears open to truth made real by Wisdom;
   with eyes open to beauty made visible by discernment;
   with delight that we are called by the voice of God's Holy Spirit.

## Invocation
### (PSALMS)

Awe-inspiring God, we of the earth sing of your glory. Our songs join with the hosts of heaven to magnify your holy name. From the mouths of children singing your praises comes the strength we need to stand firm in our faith. No vexing spirit can overwhelm us. Come, let your glory resound in our ears and hearts this day. Reveal your light through our faces and hands and feet as we sing. Bring your own joy into our voices and your peace into our silence. Come empower us to praise you. Make us the instruments of your glory throughout the earth.

## Time of Reconciliation
### (PSALMS)
### *Call to Confession*

So often the pettiness of our life overwhelms us. We become despairing of ever being free of vexation. Irritation in our life can turn us inward to brood on all the little things that make our life on this planet irksome. For turning our backs on God's magnificent glory, we ask forgiveness.

### *Confession*

O God, while above this day, the heavens in your majesty chant of glory and
   splendor . . .

I fashion the hand-jerk gesture, lurid epithet, and horn-blast salute on my
   commute.
I loose the maddening shriek over unrinsed toothpaste spit in the sink.
I mutter the predictable whine about emptying the trash.
I stew in the sullen silence of a seasoned pouter when I'm left out, not
   invited, not included.
I slam the door to make my point to the dog.

O God, hear my sorrow in my confession; forgive my being servant to trivial
pursuits. Amen.

## Assurance of Grace

God crowns us with glory and honor; we only need to look up at the heavens to
remember our crown as God's own fingers fashion it. When we turn back to
God's magnificence, we will find inspiration for our life. When we turn back to
our role of hand-helping and foot-guiding for all God's creatures under the
heavens, we will find our pettiness forgiven.

## Time of Reconciliation

### (ROMANS)

### Call to Confession

Even our faith itself is sometimes twisted. Let us confess the sin of our religion
against the reality of suffering.

### Confession

Crucified, compassionate, companion Christ—
we have offered platitudes to others
suggesting that suffering and death are God's will or their fault.
We have believed that God has a plan for individual lives
that includes illness, accident, and cruel misfortunes,
and we have worshiped an idol of divine sadism.
We have not walked with our own suffering
and experienced fully all that it could teach us,
nor have we let it help us grow.
Sometimes we have embraced suffering
and allowed it to take over our identity,
and sometimes we have fled from it
through pain-killers and alcohol.
We have not let suffering simply be a part of life
and, therefore, part of our ultimate hope in your love.
Forgive us and guide us through the painful contradiction
of your power and your love. Amen.

## Assurance of Grace

God's love has been poured into our hearts through the Holy Spirit. Christ's death sustains us in all times and an honest faith leads us to peace.

# PRAYER BEYOND THE CHURCH
### *Prayer with Elementary School Teachers*
#### (PSALMS)

When I look at the children,
I see that each one
is crowned with glory and honor,
and, while they are certainly
not angels,
they are your very image.

I teach them to look
at the heavens—
the moon and the stars,
and I want to teach them
to reach their small fingers
for the stars, too.
Can I teach them
how precious they are,
how sacred their caretaking
will be of earth and animals,
birds of the air,
forests and rivers,
and whatever passes
along the paths of the sea?

They come to me, each one
a tightly woven trinity,
of child's body-mind,
parents' influence, and a
waking wondering spirit.

Empower me, O God,
to protect their bodies
and open their minds,
to be alert to the signs
of abuse and neglect,
to be aware of the stifling
of culture, the damage
of gender-bashing,
the fragility of family.

Empower me, O God,
even in the middle of
overcrowded classrooms,
shortage of crayons,
too-old textbooks,
out-of-tune pianos,
snow days,
chicken pox seasons,
mornings when the
gerbils die,
to whisper into each
free holy spirit

that out of the mouths
of such children as these
the word of the future,
the majestic, sovereign
naming of life itself
for all your creatures,
is crying out
from the desks
of my classroom.

The preceding materials use the readings for Trinity Sunday, First Sunday after Pentecost, Year C.

# A Season for Loss

(1 KINGS 17:8–24; LUKE 7:11–17)

❖ ✄ ❖

## PRAYER OF THE HEART
### (1 KINGS)
*"Do not be afraid." (1 Kings 17:13b)*

A handful of meal,
a jug of oil,
a breath of life,
a note of song,
half a smile from a friend,
a letter folded and
refolded again,
pine needles under feet,
the smell of city
after long rain,
a child's prayer—
the little enough.

I was just going
to kindle these bits
left of my life
and consume
my last hope,
but you came along

asking me to give
rather than give up,
and I decided
to share my
next-to-nothing
with your hunger.

Taste my sweet cake
even though it is small,
taste tomorrow
with me—I think
there is enough.
Something shared
is never empty;
something poured
will never run out—
a table of meal,
a laughter of oil,
a handful of life.

## BIBLE STUDY
## Creative Encounter with the Text for a Small Group
### Option: Memory Quilt
#### (1 KINGS, LUKE)

This exercise helps us feel mourning and loss, the sadness of the two women central to these stories. Most people know about the six-foot squares of the AIDS quilt, designed to remember those who have died by illustrating those things that were important to them. Have each person take a square of white paper. With crayons and colored pencils design a quilt square for someone who is loved and is dead. Use detail in the drawing. Afterwards, describe the person and the intimate designs remembered and chosen.

## Option: Scarcity Meal
### (I KINGS)

If the exercise above, of being in touch with grief, is too difficult for the group at this time, focus on the early verses of the I Kings scripture. Make a meal together—cornbread (made with meal and oil) and "stone" soup. Have each participant take responsibility for one ingredient. Discuss what it is like to fear "running out" of the things we need.

## Suggested Questions for Discussion or Personal Reflection
### (I KINGS 17:8–24)

Identify the times in your life when you have felt at the end of your resources—meal, oil, or rope. What happened then?

When does an act of generosity replenish your own resources?

What that is precious to you seems to have died?

How deep is your intercession? Can you throw yourself on someone else's child and beg life?

Can you name your feelings to God when someone you loves is ill or dies? Can you tell another human being more easily?

What proves God's word?

### (LUKE 7:11–17)

What is the compassion of God?

Are some relationships more vital than others? Do some people need relationships more than others do?

Why does raising from the dead engender fear?

Why is the death of children so terrible?

## RESOURCES FOR CONGREGATIONAL WORSHIP
## Call to Worship
### (I KINGS, LUKE)

**One voice:** We come to worship with our sense of inadequate resources and fear for the future.

**Congregation:** And God blesses our possibilities into amazing bounty.

**One voice:** We come to worship with sadness, grief, and worry about those dear to us.

**Congregation:** God welcomes our intercession and strengthens those for whom we pray.

**One voice:** We come to worship with ourselves—imperfect, awkward, and unsure.

**Congregation:** And we discover that God is waiting for us, longing for us, loving us and willing us to love ourselves.

## Invocation

Gracious God, we come to this holy hour with our own lonely silences and loud distractions. Let us know your whisper in the midst of all that clutters our spirits. Reach into the center of our souls with the peace, courage, patience, acceptance, or forgiveness we all need, and then open us to the incredible blessing which is the presence of one another. Amen.

## Time of Reconciliation

### Call to Confession

There is a chasm in us which separates us from compassion. Words span the emptiness, and our hearts follow.

### Confession

Gentle God, hear our sins and have mercy on us.

> Forgive us the words we have said which have given pain, and
> the words we have left unsaid which might have given hope.
> Forgive us the actions we have taken which have harmed
> friend or stranger, and the things undone which
> could have made a difference.
> Forgive us the thoughts which poison ourselves and
> deprecate others, and the thoughtlessness
> which ignores caring and worship.

Gentle God, have mercy on us and give us peace. Amen.

### Assurance of Grace

When we cross over the bridge within ourselves which is confession, we discover that we are at home with God. To dwell there quietly is to know forgiveness.

## PRAYER BEYOND THE CHURCH

### Prayer with Parents Who Have Lost Children

(I KINGS, LUKE)

This is a grief
like no other grief,
and yet we are very different—
some of us have children
who have died literally—
younger or older,
or still in the womb—
by accident or illness,
by murder or by their
own hands.

Others of us have children
somewhere still alive,
but dead to us—
children in foster homes,
children who are angry,
children who are
strangled by addiction,
children we gave up for adoption
long ago, and now we wait,
hoping they'll seek
our names.

Some have believed the hatred
of our ex-spouses,
or truly remembered
the harm we did.
Some have married men
and women who do not like us.
Some have chosen religions
that drive them from us,
or philosophies that we
cannot share.
Some are in prison,
or in comas,
or busy with their own
children and grandchildren,
too busy for us. . . .

All of these are different losses,
but they all feel like death.
It doesn't matter
if we have other children,
it doesn't matter
if it's been many years—
it is still a grief
like no other grief
and there is hollowness
when others speak of children.

We flee the holidays,
we burn photographs . . .
or enshrine them.
The sight of babies in the park
makes us cry,
and we want to scream
at mothers and fathers
who don't take time
every day
to hug their boys and girls.

God, receive our rage and pain
and our self-pity.
Let us sob in you
the deep silent tears
that others think are finished
and batter reproaches
harmlessly against you
that would kill us
if we turned them inward.
And when we are resigned
to the burying of love—
surprise some of us
with a child
brought back to life,
a second chance, and
open others to someone else's
hurting child
who needs to be loved,

God, let all of us
find some peaceful forgettings
and peaceful rememberings,
a good friend to listen
to our story again,
and, at last, a still place
within ourselves
where we can discover
that there is more
in us than people
who live their lives
to weep.

The preceding materials use readings from the season of Pentecost, Year C.

# A Season of Grace

(PSALM 5:1–8; LUKE 7:36–8:3)

## PRAYER OF THE HEART
### (LUKE)

*"And a woman in the city, who was a sinner, having learned that he was eating in the Pharisee's house, brought an alabaster jar of ointment."*
*(Luke 7:37)*

God of invitation,
Do you come
to set a table
for your grace?
With open fare
to all made plain—
works of wonder,
words of dominion,
acts of healing,
kindness steadfast
leading footsteps
back to love—
who comes to
sit with you
and eat?

As one,
a woman nameless
does—
do we?
Have we a name
that's soiled with life's
untidy stains?
Have we a heart
That grieves our
body's pain
and God's lost soul?
Do we, as she—

lay down the cloak of shame
untie the bonds of guilt
and come to taste
your grace?

Have we gnawed
enough at life
to tell
what
makes a feast
of love?
Have we lost
enough of self-esteem
to sell what's left
for oil
and with it wipe
the feet of God?
Would Love
refuse?

Touching God
is real.
We've missed
the realness
all these years
of touching
what we
thought

| was God. | for the touch |
|---|---|
| Release | restored. |
| the tears of sorrow | Forgiveness is |
| for our missing | found |
| touch. | in flesh |
| Release | made real |
| the tears of joy | by touch. |

# BIBLE STUDY
## Creative Encounter with the Text for a Small Group
### *Looking for Love*
#### (LUKE)

Sit at a table with several different sizes/shapes/colors of containers: flasks, jars, bottles, cups. Invite each one present to select one container and share the grace of God contained in it with the group.

## Suggested Questions for Discussion or Personal Reflection
### (PSALM 5:1–8)

Where do you go to meet God's grace?
When are you ready for God's grace?
How do you communicate with God?
Who lies between you and God's grace?
Why would God listen to you?

### (LUKE 7:36–8.3)

How has God's grace changed your life?
Where have you waited for God's grace?
What extravagant gesture of thanks have you made to God?
When have you wept in gratitude for God's forgiveness?
How do you prepare to thank God?
Whose feet have you kissed?
How do you know you're forgiven?

# RESOURCES FOR CONGREGATIONAL WORSHIP
## Call to Worship
### (PSALMS)

**One voice:** Before whose ears have we come to speak in prayer?
**Congregation:** We come with words of prayer to speak before our God.
**One voice:** Who will listen to our voices today?
**Congregation:** Our God, who brings in the new day, listens for our prayers in the morning.

**One voices:** Who is welcome to pray in God's house?

**Congregation:** All who truly struggle with evil are welcome to pray here.

**One voice:** How have we each come through the doors of God's praying house?

**Congregation:** We have come into this house of prayer by the greatness of God's love for us.

## Invocation

### (PSALMS)

In the plenty of grace, O God, we come to you. Draw us along the path of life that leads to your waiting embrace. We call upon you this day to listen to the words of our mouth and the sighs of our hearts. They are cries for help. Make room for us in your house of prayer, for we are set upon by worldly ways of iniquity and deceit. Alone we waver, not knowing your way plainly. Accept us as your own, for we reverence your name. Hear our growing desire for you to be the center of our life. We look to you. Please make your way clear before us this day. In Christ's name, we pray. Amen.

## Time of Reconciliation

### (PSALMS, LUKE)

### *Call to Confession*

Through love we come to love.
Bowing, we seek to stand.
Confessing, we stumble into righteousness.

### *Confession*

Forgive me that I have not loved enough.
Forgive me so that I can love you and others,
    no matter what their sins may be.
Forgive me that I have not fully believed
    in the possibility and power of forgiveness.
Forgive me so that I can forgive—
    others and myself. Amen.

### *Assurance of Grace*

The faith of our seeking grace has saved us. Love extravagantly. Be in peace.

# Prayer beyond the Church

*Prayer with Rapists, Pedophiles, and Clergy and Therapists Who Have Sexually Violated the Trust Placed in Them*

(LUKE)

I am not welcome in the church—
no one is interested in
the victim in me,
or the human.
No one believes my rehabilitation—
I don't expect them to.
But I reach out my fingers
to this scripture
and you know
who is touching you.

This scripture isn't about women.
It's about someone
whose kisses
were unholy
kissing your feet.
It's about loosening
my disheveled history,
offering my shame
and my gift,
listening to murmurs
of outrage,
and weeping
terrible tears.

It's about my
terrible sin and my
terrible love,
and your
terrible
forgiveness,

and being sent away
in peace.

The preceding materials use readings from the season of Pentecost, Year C.

# A Season of Loneliness

(I KINGS 19:1–15A; PSALMS 42, 43; GALATIANS 3:23–29;
LUKE 8:26–39)

❖ ✄ ❖

## PRAYER OF THE HEART

### (LUKE)

*"As he stepped out on land, a man of the city who had demons met him."*
*(Luke 8:27)*

Soul-seeing God,
out beyond the haven walls
of safety and repute
are holes for foxes, adders
and the dead.
There the outcast lives
among the tombs,
outlawed and homeless
as the villain civil strife.
Not much to lure you
for a sight.
Why have you come?
Are you in search of what
cannot be tamed:
my body's lost restraint?
my mind's abandoned sense?
my soul's long-buried light?
my spirit's unclean scent?

What do you want with me, Jesus,
Child of the Most High God?
No chain yet built
can hold me
to a common life.
And yet I would be seen.
Even now
amongst these tombs
that stare unseeing
into my face
I live.
My need's for sight:
for being seen
by eyes that long
for wild release,
by eyes that see
not tombs
but life.
Tame me, gentle God.
Tame my wildest,
outcast self.

## BIBLE STUDY

Creative Encounter with the Text for a Small Group
*New Hope among Epitaphs*

### (LUKE)

In a central dish of sand, distribute at random several "tomb" stones. Ask each
person present to select from baskets of colored glass, shells, semiprecious stones,
dried flowers and spices, etc., some object(s) to place in the sand dish among

the tombstones. Let the chosen object represent some piece of his or her life that feels left out, homeless, or exiled from the community of faith. Share what it represents with the group after all have placed their objects in the sand. Add objects or reconfigure the scene, after all have shared their stories, to represent how the elements might become a garden.

## Suggested Questions for Discussion or Personal Reflection

### (1 KINGS 19:1–15A)

From whom are you fleeing for your life?

Where do you go when you flee?

How is God present in your flight?

What is God asking you to find?

### (PSALMS 42, 43)

When do you thirst for God?

What invites you to feel exiled from God?

How is your thirst quenched?

When do you find God?

### (GALATIANS 3:23–29)

How do you wear Christ?

Does Christ fit?

Where is Christ threadbare in your life?

How does Christ's community without distinction call us to have an impact on our world?

### (LUKE 8:26–39)

What part of your life lives outside the land of the living? What imprisons you there?

What does Jesus want with that part of your life?

What is the cost of leaving your place of exile?

## RESOURCES FOR CONGREGATIONAL WORSHIP
## Call to Worship
### (PSALMS)

**One voice:** God's truth shines in the light of a new day!

**Congregation:** We come wanting God's truth to be our guide.

**One voice:** God's truth leads us to a place of holiness and light.

**Congregation:** We come wanting God's truth to be our home.

**One voice:** God's truth lives in songs of praise and joy!

**Congregation:** We come wanting God's truth to be our feast.

**One voice:** God's truth deepens our life as our thirst for God deepens.

**Congregation:** We come thirsty for God's truth.

We come thirsty for God.

We come thankfully to drink from the well of God's grace, that God's truth may live in us.

## Invocation

### (KINGS)

God of sustaining grace, come be with us. We are flee-ers, runaways from fear, refugees of the soul! Send your angel to touch us. Free us from the power of demons that would chase us to despair. Take away the nightmare of unending flight. Come to our deserted hearts and fill them with peace. With your hand feed us trust. Breathe hope into our souls. Lead our body of flesh onward to a life of servant love without fear. Transform our furze-tree spirit of gloom into an eager walk. Amen.

## Time of Reconciliation

### (GALATIANS)

### *Call to Confession*

God calls us to step out from under old reliable guardians of our connection with God to choose new relationships with God based on faith. For clinging to our old ways of certainty, for fear of new and improbable ways of faith, let us repent.

### *Confession*

God of mercy, we are hard-pressed to loosen grips on self-preserving rules. A sure and present guardian is your law which keeps our differences defined. Separate and apart we need not fear the unknown voice of something alien and strange. We need not tap the blind one's stick nor veil the leper's shame. Forgive our need to hide from what we fear. Hear our hearts confess that we have clung to what the law in letters can provide: a reason to exclude. Forgive, we pray, our sin of self-enamored sight. Help us offer our life to being clothed in Christ. Accept our new intent to put on fully the cloak of Christ and walk in servant love. Let all who see us come, see Christ. Amen.

### *Assurance of Grace*

Belonging to Christ clothes us through our faith in the promises of the one true God of Love.

# Prayer beyond the Church

*Prayer with People with Anorexia*

### (1 kings)

I am alone and I want to die;
I am alone and I try to die.
It is an angel who makes me
get up and eat;
it is an angel
who wakes me up
a second time and
makes me eat,
and a third time
and, on this terrible journey,
more than forty times.

An angel in a hospital,
when all I wanted
was my cave.

In my cave I hear a great wind,
so strong it breaks mountains,
and this wind is self-hatred
and looking
in the magazines,
and looking in the mirror,
and seeing my ugly bulk,
my fat, my awkward
lumpiness.
In my cave I smell a fire.
Fire is always in control,
and I want to control
something, anything.
I want to control my body,
I want to control
my parents.
In my cave I feel
an earthquake—
and I am frightened,
and I try to be a child again,
and I become smaller

and smaller,
because I know
when I am small enough
someone will protect me.
But God is not in the self-hatred,
and God is not in the control,
and God is not in
the child-making
that is killing me.

But after that there is a place
and a time
of sheer silence,
and I come to the entrance
with my face shielded
for fear of losing
everything of me,
but I discover that
I am not the wind,
I am not the fire,
I am not the earthquake. . . .

I am
the deep, sweet, God-soaked
silence,
I am my body—
more than bones,
I am menstrual again,
beautiful—
and I am not alone.

Thanks to the angel
I have lived long enough
to walk out of
the cave.

The preceding materials use readings from the season of Pentecost, Year C.

# A Season of Holy Touchings

## (2 SAMUEL 1:1–27; MARK 5:21–43)

### PRAYER OF THE HEART
#### (MARK)

*"Immediately aware that power had gone forth from him, Jesus turned about in the crowd and said, 'Who touched my clothes?'" (Mark 5:34)*

Was it a tumor in her uterus that made her bleed so long?
Was it an abortion she regretted that would never go away?
Was she beaten every day,
or did she hurt herself?

I do not know, gentle God,
what made this woman so desperate
she would touch a strange man in the street—
But I feel my own reaching. . . .

Was it anorexia that killed the teenage girl?
Was it self-doubt, pregnancy, or fear of growing up too soon?
Was it loneliness, responsibility, or did she hate her body?

I do not know, gentle God,
what laid this girl so still that a
death-raiser had to come to her—
But I feel my own powerlessness. . . .

Desperate or powerless—
    sometimes I reach out for the fabric
    of your garment, silent, furtive with hope,
    choking the words I dare not say.
    sometimes another must intercede for me,
    entreat and bring your presence
    to the bed where I am paralyzed.

When I am desperate, Savior, offer me peace.
When I am powerless, teach those I love to feed me.
Amen.

# Bible Study
## Creative Encounter with the Text for a Small Group
### *Touching the Fringe*
#### (Mark)

Have several coats hanging around the room—a homeless person's coat, a pastor's robe, a grandmother's shawl, a doctor's white lab coat, a small angel costume from the Christmas pageant, etc. Explain at the beginning that these represent Jesus' garment in the passage from Mark, and that we believe we experience Christ walking through our lives in the garments of others. Invite each participant to take an opportunity at some point during the class to go to one of the coats, hold it, and pray for healing—for oneself or in intercession for someone else. Discuss the day's questions, but save fifteen minutes at the end to ask how people felt about these moments of prayer for healing.

## Suggested Questions for Discussion or Personal Reflection
### (2 Samuel 1:1, 17–27, the lectionary selection)

Have you ever grieved for someone who was your "enemy"?

David says that Jonathan's love was more wonderful to him than the love of women. What do you think characterized their relationship?

How do we honor/cherish relationships between people of the same gender?

### (Read also: 2 Samuel 1:2–16)

How do you respond to the story of the death of the Amalekite?

This is clearly a case of mercy killing for Saul, who had failed to commit suicide. How do you feel about assisted suicide?

### (Mark 5:21–43)

Do you believe in Jesus' power to heal?

How are people with chronic illnesses—physical and mental illnesses—treated as unclean in our society?

What are sacred things you can touch?

How does our faith heal us?

What miracles have you experienced as interruptions?

What kills twelve-year-old girls in our society?

## Resources for Congregational Worship
### Call to Worship

**One voice:** Let us worship God in the community called church.

**Congregation:** We can worship God on the seashore or a mountaintop, but it gives us joy to be together.

**One voice:** Let us pray to God in the community called church.

**Congregation:** We can pray by dinner tables or hospital beds, while we are working or taking a walk, but we feel peace when we pray together.

**One voice:** Let us serve God in the community called church.

**Congregation:** We can serve God at the homeless shelter or the ballot box, or every time we help a neighbor, but we are stronger when we serve together.

## Invocation
### (2 SAMUEL, MARK)

Gentle God, some of us gather to prayer from grieving moods or hurting bodies, from fear or loss or pain. Others of us gather to prayer from joy, excitement and hope. We bring you a harmony of lives, a rainbow of feelings, a community of mutual support and profound worship. Amen.

## Time of Reconciliation
### (MARK)
### *Call to Confession*

God calls us from the crowd and hears the stories that tremble on our lips. Let us pray in confession.

### *Confession*

Gentle God, we bring before you our burdens, our long-standing misgivings about ourselves and our need for reconciliation when we are isolated from others. You know how we have failed to live up to our own expectations and walk in your path. Our thoughts, words, and deeds have been barriers to your love, and we have not been willing to reach across them. Help us to look honestly at ourselves, experience true repentance, touch your healing, and remake damaged relationships with others. Amen.

### *Assurance of Grace*

God affirms our confession—our faith has made us well; we may go in peace.

## PRAYER BEYOND THE CHURCH
*Prayer with People Who Have Lost Those They Love of the Same Gender\**
### (2 SAMUEL)

Wrap the quilt of your comfort
around my shoulders.
I have lost my wonderful love,
my friend, my partner,
the person who was
the miracle in my life,
the bread-with companion,
the surprise.
Our endearments were not
the smooth sentiments of
greeting-card verse,

but we were dear in other words.
Some people walked away from us,
and we held hands sadly
to watch them go.
Our moments of
ordinary tenderness—
the breakfast flowers
and the shore walking,
dancing to the radio,
Christmas presents, and
laughter—

\*Some of these are gay, lesbian, and bisexual people; others have lived many years with one friend.

were very precious,
more precious to us,
more chosen,
than the expected familiar
of husband and wife.

Now there is death
and the empty chair.
Now the raised eyebrows
at the funeral parlor,

and looking down the
corridor of solitude.

You hear me cry, gentle God,
and you understand
all the loss and loneliness.
Your tears mingle with mine,
with memories—

Jonathan,
Naomi,
Lazarus. Amen.

## PRAYER BEYOND THE CHURCH
### *Prayer in a Situation of Assisted Suicide*
#### (2 SAMUEL 1:2–16)

God,
hear my prayer
for nurses, doctors,
nursing home health aides,
cousins, children,
spouses, friends,
and all the other
loving, hurting, lonely,
world-condemned
Amalekites.

Some time, some place,
someone we never
expected to say it,
said,
"Come, stand over
me and kill me,
for my life
still lingers."
And we did it,
and ran away
with our clothes torn
and dirt on our heads
for the bad dying,
the terrible choice,
the broken-hearted fear
that we may have been
wrong.

We may have been wrong.

All the world recoils
from the danger of us.

We are the alien ones,
the specter-possibility of
convenient death,
of ruthless power.
And we have stirred
the spirit-deep
hatred
of the living
for suicide.

But we must claim fully
both the mercy
and the killing,
and stand
in the presence
of the sorrow of God,
because we have faith
that God knows
more about both
killing and mercy
than David,
or anyone else,
ever can—
and that God will walk
with us through
the valley of the shadow
of some else's death,
and will not call us evil,
but will hold our
bloody, loving
hands.

The preceding materials use readings from the season of Pentecost, Year B.

# House-Building and Healing

(2 SAMUEL 7:1–14A; EPHESIANS 2:11–22;
MARK 6:30–34, 53–56)

❖ ✄ ❖

## PRAYER OF THE HEART
### (MARK)

*"When they had crossed over, they came to land at Gennesaret and moored
the boat." (Mark 6:53)*

Swineherds said it best, my God:
   "He gave the madman back his life!"
With just a word from him, they said,
   the demons let the wild man go and seized the pigs instead.
They saw a whole man left, well and sane and fully clothed.
The healer sent the new man home to live a normal life,
   to tell what had been done for him.
They said his people, when they heard what happened, came in fear,
   to beg the healer-man get out and leave them as they were.

My God, what is this madness inside me that bids me
   go to see the man who heals?
No chain-snapping demons possess my mind; I have
   no withered hand or crippled feet,
   no leprosy, no issue of blood,
   no daughter desperately ill;
What need have I to see the man who heals?

My God, would I care not where I go in order to be with him:
   for the sight of him alone?
   for just the thrill?
   to hear his voice?
   to speak with him?
   to watch another healing?
   to get some bread?

My God, I'd go to change my life.
   I'd go to find a wholeness that I lack.
   I'd go to feel a wellness that I want.
   I'd go to take a Savior that I need.

My God, I'd go to give him thanks that he leaves no one as they were.
"He gives all the madmen back their lives!"
This is the prayer of a first-century witness to the healing of the Gerasene demoniac.

# BIBLE STUDY
## Creative Encounter with the Text for a Small Group
### *House-Building*
#### (2 SAMUEL, EPHESIANS)

Ask each person present to contribute one small item from his or her posses-sions that day to construct a cross in the middle of a large dish of sand. From baskets of several varieties of small sticks and stones, invite people then to build together a house for God on top of or around that cross. Ask all participants to reflect on a thought or feeling that they experience as they do this or as they sit back and ponder what they have done (or what Christ has done) as a member of a community.

## Suggested Questions for Discussion or Personal Reflection
### (2 SAMUEL 7:1–14A)

What part of shepherding do you do well?
What have you built to house God's sheep?
What place have you provided for God to live in you?

### (EPHESIANS 2:11–22)

What barrier separates you from the love of God?
What keeps you from accepting Christ's cross as the way to God's love?
Where do you fit in the house where God lives?

### (MARK 6:30–34, 53–56)

What place in you remains shepherdless?
How do you recognize a true shepherd?
How do you touch God's healing power?

# RESOURCES FOR CONGREGATIONAL WORSHIP
## Call to Worship
### (2 SAMUEL)

**One voice:** Are we a people to build God a house to dwell in today?
**Congregation:** God has taken us from wandering in the wilderness of our doubt to this place.
God has guided us safely in all our journeys through adversity to this place.
God has planted us in a fertile land and granted us peace.
God has made us into a house where the holy name of God may live.
**One voice:** Thanks be to God who comes to dwell in us today!

## Invocation

Tent-dweller God, you have lived in many places. You know the weariness of continually packing up and moving on. Many of us have traveled far in search of how to be at home with you. Our bodies are tired. Our souls seek rest. Come help us stop this wandering after you into houses that others have built. Help us accept that you do indeed dwell in buildings unlike ours; but open our eyes to see that you also live in us. Make a home of us where we both can dwell in peace.

## Time of Reconciliation

(EPHESIANS)

### Call to Confession

When we find ourselves far off and alienated from membership in God's household, we suffer injustice. For those places where we have been cut off from God's body, or for those places where we have cut off another from full membership in the household of God, we are sorry and humbly repent.

### Confession

We ask forgiveness for closed doors in our body of Christ and household of God:
- . . . that exclude people with special mobility needs from attending church with dignity.
- . . . that exclude people of a different race or nationality from leadership positions.
- . . . that exclude people of new language sensibilities from influencing worship.
- . . . that exclude people from communion because they are too young.
- . . . that exclude babies from being baptized because their parents are not members.
- . . . that exclude from social fellowship people of different sexual orientation.

Amen.

### Assurance of Grace

Those who come to God in genuine regret for the barriers they have met or helped erect in order to build God's household to suit a human design, God mercifully forgives. Christ's own body is the entrance to the household of God. All who enter through Christ will be welcome and find a home.

# PRAYER BEYOND THE CHURCH
## Prayer with People in Construction Trades
### (2 SAMUEL, EPHESIANS)

On Sunday in church
I hear my work as a metaphor—
building a house for God
is something done in our hearts or
in the caring of communities.
Sometimes our bodies themselves
are temples built for God.

But it's real for me—
building a house for God—
carpentry, masonry, electricity,
    plumbing—
every house for a family
is really a house for God.
Every small office building
for doctors, dentists, lawyers,
    therapists
is a place people will bring
their needs and hopes.
And in the supermarket,
mounded with grapefruit and
    lettuce,
filled with pork chops and toilet
    paper,
with toddlers begging for sugared
    cereal,
with two-inch-high headlines
and horoscopes,
there throbs more energy and living
than in most sanctuaries.
Even the mall where teenagers flirt
and elderly cardiac patients
walk miles for health and
    friendship
is a kind of sacred place
where strangers gather
and brush one another

and the lights are bright
against these lonely times.
And on the unfinished high-rise
with its winds and girder
    camaraderie,
when I stand up in the sky—
blue or gray
or gold burning that pink color
from the inside of sea shells—
I know I touch heaven.

Not all the moments
are so holy.
It's also real in sweaty heat and cold rain,
in the danger of falling
that has taken friends' lives.
There are crude jokes and hard feelings
at some sites about women in the trades
or college kids who set themselves apart
or try to get too close,
and there are long days waiting for work,
and too much drinking,
and a body early-old in joints
and missing fingers.

In the metaphor
remember those.

But remember most
where spiritual and real come true—
my pride in looking
at a place I made,
at some tabernacle idea
that became cedar and stone,
at a dwelling made with hands
that were my hands—
and now God lives there.

The preceding materials use readings from the season of Pentecost, Year B.

# Sisters and Prophets

(AMOS 8:1–12; COLOSSIANS 1:15–28; LUKE 10:38–42)

## PRAYER OF THE HEART
### (LUKE)

*"Martha, Martha, you are worried and distracted by many things."*
*(Luke 10:41b)*

There is a part of each of us
named Martha which
tends the needs of others with
competence and compassion until
the nerve-ends of our own neediness
are vulnerable and exposed.

That Martha-part appears to ripen and
yet is sometimes only a swollen seed.
A famine gnaws within our own self-worth
because we think our work
is how we meet our needs.

Kind Traveler God, who rests a
gentle guest in Martha's home,
you are willing to stay with each one of us,
when we welcome you to our homes.
Help us to ask you in, blessing Christ,
bearing your precious gift.

Gentle Guest, set down your blessing gift—
the gift of calling us by name
and not by what we do,
the gift of unraveling
our knot of unmet needs,
the gift of offering us again
life's good parts to choose.

Set us free from distracting worry, toil,
resentment, scolding discontent.
Set us as free as your host friend Martha

to find it's not the serving,
but the God,
who meets our needs.

Then, help us, gentle Guest,
to see we each one let you in,
when at the heart of what we do
to serve you best
lies our small chosen act of surrender
to the peace that comes with you as host
and we as joyful guests.

# Bible Study
## Creative Encounter with the Text for a Small Group
### *Hymn-Bring*
#### (colossians)

Part of this passage in Colossians is an early Christian hymn—complex, mysterious, and beautiful. Have all the participant bring in the text to their favorite hymns. Have them share—as much as they can—why they like the hymns and what the hymns mean to them. Consider the variety of the theological perspectives and the emotional depth of the hymns. Music is a vital part of the effectiveness of hymns. Sing some of the hymns. Discuss how the music affects the theology.

## Suggested Questions for Discussion or Personal Reflection
### (amos 8:1–12)

What do you think of when you see a basket of summer fruit?

What is the result to a society of abusing the poor?

How does contemporary society use "false balances," and cheat on the Sabbath for profit?

How does our contemporary society "sell" the poor people in our midst?

How does God respond to our participation in corporate selfishness?

What would a famine of hearing the words of God be?

### (colossians 1:15–28)

Is this passage theology or poetry? How does this appeal to intellect? to emotion?

How is Christ a part of creation?

How is Christ a part of salvation and reconciliation?

What is the maturity in Christ for which we are striving? What is your next step of growth?

What distracts you from listening to God?

How do you best serve God?

What conflicts have you had with sisters/brothers?

# RESOURCES FOR CONGREGATIONAL WORSHIP
## Call to Worship
### (COLOSSIANS)

**One voice:** We come to Christ—image of the invisible God.

**Congregation:** In Christ is the creation of all things in heaven and earth, thrones or dominions, rulers or powers.

**One voice:** We come to Christ in whom all things hold together.

**Congregation:** In Christ is the church, the fullness of God, the possibility of the Resurrection.

**One voice:** We come to Christ, in whose cross is found reconciliation for all things.

**Congregation:** In Christ is profound peace—from hostility, from division, from sin and even death itself.

## Invocation
### (LUKE)

Journeying God, come into our house and find welcome here. Draw each of us to sit at your feet and listen to your words. Help us set aside all that would distract us from receiving you. Center our restless minds; soothe our anxious hearts; quiet our overwrought bodies; call to our thirsty souls. Dear Christ, be gentle with us as we are, and lead us to the better part of life which you have in mind for us today. Amen.

## Time of Reconciliation
### (AMOS)
### *Call to Confession*

We often focus on the individual dimensions of reconciliation and abdicate responsibility for the social injustices that undergird our comfortable standard of living. When we do not practice repentance for participation in this sinfulness, we are lulled away from any urgent call to change our society.

### *Confession*

Fierce, justice-seeking God—
We confess to you that we have oppressed the needy
and contributed to the ruin of women and children,
the poorest in our midst.

We confess that we have tolerated unscrupulous business practices
and have condoned the violence of governments.
We confess that we have masked ruthlessness or indifference
with church-going and civic virtue and have been
unwilling to listen to your demands for reparation.
Call us to repentance and recommit us to changing the world. Amen.

## Assurance of Grace

We have not yet come to the famine of hearing God's word. Because we still can
hear its uncompromising demand for justice, we know we are forgiven into
responsibility.

# PRAYER BEYOND THE CHURCH
## *Prayer for Advocates of Social Justice*
### (AMOS)

You show me a basket of summer fruit—
raspberries, peaches,
nectarines, plums—
and I want to eat some and rest.
Sitting under my own grapevine
on an August evening,
I want to taste the sweetness,
dripping down my chin.

I do not want one more metaphor
for prophecy—
an image of ripe death, of people-
    harvest.
I am tired of preaching about the pain
of the oppressed to the comfortable
about the trampling down of the needy
to those who blame them for their needs.
I am tired of castigating the hypocrisy
of church and state, weary of
boiling with righteousness and
anger and truth.

What more can I threaten?
the globe-shadowing
of corporate greed?
the coming of a time when poor
    children
will rise up in indiscriminate
    violence
on street corners, and the sound
of crying will be heard in the
    kitchens
where we danced to radio tunes?

I repeat myself and people laugh
    at me.
But now I feel the famine creeping in
and closing my throat—
not a famine of bread or a
thirst for water, but a
famine for hearing the word of God.

For when you devour the fruit of
    hope,
you become very hungry.

The preceding materials use readings from the season of Pentecost, Year C.

# Small Metaphor and Extravagant Promise

## (ROMANS 8:26–39; MATTHEW 13:31–33, 44–52)

### PRAYER OF THE HEART
#### (MATTHEW)

*"Jesus told the crowds all these things in parables; without parable he told them nothing." (Matthew 13:34)*

Come to me bulldozing God,
and treasure my field,
full of artifacts and potatoes.
Dig the hidden
holiness
in the ordinary soil.

Come to me bird-watching God,
you will find the branches
for nesting.
A mustard seed of faith
grows to a place
of many wings.

Come to me fish-netting God,
cast your wide love which
draws in without judgment.
All fish written
in the dirt
are a sign for Christ.

Come to me bread-baking God,
give yeast for my rising,
knead the warm dough.
Bake the sweet smell
that always sings
the end of hunger.

Come to me pearl-hunting God,
dive my depths,
open my shell.
Find the place of past intrusion
where translucent beauty forms layers
around sharp pain.

Come to me parable-telling God,
metaphor-lavish
with images to say you love me,
until your word-palette
paints new meaning
into my life.

### BIBLE STUDY
## Creative Encounter with the Text for a Small Group
### *Writing a Parable*
#### (MATTHEW)

Write a parable. Here are three ways to start the group writing parables:

1. Ask participants to tell a story of something that happened this week. Does it point to a larger meaning? If they changed the ending, would it point to a different meaning?

2. Fill a table with objects. Have each person choose an object and observe a parallel truth. For example, one might choose a candle and observe that prayer is like a candle: it lights up the dark, although it doesn't make the morning come sooner.

3. Suggest that they begin with an idea they've always wanted to express. Have them think of something concrete to which it could be compared.

## Suggested Questions for Discussion or Personal Reflection
### (ROMANS 8:26–39)

How does the Spirit pray in us when we cannot pray?

"We know that all things work together for good for those who love God, according to [God's] purpose" (Romans 8:28). How is the preceding verse used in damaging ways?

What things do you think are "predestined"? How is predestination a comfort?

Is there anything that can separate us from the love of God in Christ?

Is the affirmation of Romans 8:31–39 more clearly understood in good times or hard times? Why?

### (MATTHEW 13:31–33, 44–52)

Why is the realm of heaven like a mustard seed?

What is the result of the realm of heaven "leavening" the rest of life?

How is the church like a small treasure in a lot of dirt?

What would you sell or give up for the realm of heaven?

If the realm of heaven is like a net, why should we ever turn anyone away from baptism?

Do parables make the truth easier to understand or harder to ignore?

## RESOURCES FOR CONGREGATIONAL WORSHIP
## Call to Worship
### (MATTHEW)

**One voice:** This church is a field where mustard seeds grow.

**Congregation:** Small faith is welcome here.

**One voice:** This church is a loaf where love is the leaven.

**Congregation:** And this church has a hidden treasure in its heart.

**One voice:** This church casts nets of tolerance over all people.

**Congregation:** And in this church we are pearl hunters,
even searching for holiness that grows around wounds.

# Invocation

(ROMANS)

Let the Spirit pray in us, God.
Hear the silences between our words.
As our lungs and lips breathe in and out,
may true needs,
deep longings,
unglimpsed hopes,
and paralyzing fears
be exhaled into your heart
through the Spirit's
sighing.
Amen.

163

*Small Metaphor
and Extravagant
Promise*

# Time of Reconciliation

(ROMANS)

## *Call to Confession*

God is for us, but we are often against ourselves. Let us pray in confession.

## *Confession*

Gracious God, we confess that we separate ourselves from your unconditional love. We are not willing to accept its magnificence, its freedom, and its responsibility. Instead we fill ourselves with details of life and fears of death, worries about things present and confusion about things to come. Forgive us and find us in the midst of ourselves. Amen.

## *Assurance of Grace*

God never condemns us. Christ always reaches for us. Not even our own creation can separate us from the love of God in Christ Jesus. Amen.

# PRAYER BEYOND THE CHURCH

## *Prayer at the Time of Suicide*

(ROMANS)

I don't know how to pray.
Spirit, pray.

Who is to condemn?
Spirit, pray.

While the Spirit prays to God
because of my unspeakable rage and sorrow,
I only can speak to you, my dear one.
Hear my blessing in the place
where you have gone from me:

Nothing can separate you from Christ's love—
not your life,
or your death;
not angels who did not protect you
or friends who did not hear you;
not gunshot or hunger strike,
or exhaust fumes, or sleeping pills,
or tall buildings, or subway trains,
or car crashes, or car blazings,
or bridge jumping,
or rope hanging,
or turning your face to the wall.
Not anything else in all creation
will be able to separate you
from the love of God in Christ Jesus.

Not your despair or my grief;
not your pain or my anger;
not the letter you left,
or the hearts you break;
not the past or the future;
not pity
or excuses.
Not anything else in all creation,
not you yourself—
and not God—
will ever be able to separate you
from the love of God in Christ Jesus.

The preceding materials use readings from the season of Pentecost, Year A.

# Filling the Soul Hunger

(2 KINGS 4:42–44; EPHESIANS 3:14–21; JOHN 6:1–21)

◈ ✄ ◈

## PRAYER OF THE HEART
### (EPHESIANS)

"*. . . and that Christ may dwell in your hearts through faith, as you are being rooted and grounded in love.*" *(Ephesians 3:17)*

Root me in love
like a deep tap root,
sunk in peat moss tradition,
nurture and remembering,
and the mother-care
of Spirit.

Ground me in love,
lightning rod through me
a safety against
the sudden striking

of emotional violence
and life's storms.
Root me and ground me—
yes, grow in me the hidden
dark bulb of prayer;
quiver in me vibrant
a sky-illuminating joy.
Depth and height,
earth and electricity,
dwell there Christ—
fully God, fully love.

## Creative Encounter with the Text for a Small Group
### Multiplication Tables
#### (2 KINGS, JOHN)

Ask every participant to share a "multiplication" story. There weren't enough: food, time, strength, volunteers, energy; and then suddenly, almost miraculously, there were plenty and even leftovers. Reflect not only on the stories shared, but on how stringing a lot of these stories together—hearing and celebrating them—makes the group feel.

## Suggested Questions for Discussion or Personal Reflection
### (2 KINGS 4:42–44)

How does giving anything away cause it to increase?
How does God feed us through other people?
What are the "leftovers" from the feast of God?

### (JOHN 6:1–21)

What "signs" cause you to follow Jesus?

Why is it easier to eat a miracle when we are sitting down?

What gifts that we offer to be used by other people might be multiplied by God?

When have you wanted to bring God into your "boat" (your immediate situation) but God was only willing to get you safely to your destination?

(EPHESIANS 3:14–21)

What needs to be strengthened in your "inner being"?

Name one event in life which has rooted and grounded you in love.

How do moments when you are filled with the fullness of God feel? Do such experiences turn you inward or outward?

How do we let God work within us?

Is it hard to give up control to God?

Recall a time you were able to do far more than you thought you could "ask or imagine."

## RESOURCES FOR CONGREGATIONAL WORSHIP
## Call to Worship
### (2 KINGS AND JOHN)

**One voice:** We come hungry to worship and with little in our hands.
**Congregation:** We expect to be satisfied—abundantly filled with grace.
**One voice:** We sit down together to eat a miracle.
**Congregation:** We will rise up laughing . . . and with leftovers.

## Invocation
### (EPHESIANS)

Spirit of Christ, give us love-power, and saint-power, and inner-being-power, that we may understand within ourselves the breadth and length, the height and depth of the fullness of God. Amen.

## Time of Reconciliation
### (JOHN)
### *Call to Confession*

We often set out on our journeys without Christ and then search for him in rough crossings. Let us confess our sins.

### *Confession*

God, we make life a hard rowing.
We strain in our own ways, certain
that we can plan and control the future.

God, we are storm-tossed by worry,
grief and doubt, and yet we fear you more
than familiar turbulence.

God, we try to pull you into our boats—
tame you to our expectations,
claim you for our denominations.

Calm us, still us, and bring us to the shore of your will. Amen.

### Assurance of Grace

Christ crosses our paths with peace and pardon. This is our confidence—we
never journey alone.

## PRAYER BEYOND THE CHURCH

*Prayer with Clergy*

(JOHN)

Thank you for the leftovers,
for the scraps of miracle
we gather after your gift
to this wondering multitude
who sat on the grass
and ate all they needed
from your abundance
and prayer.

We saw them come, drawn
by the rumor of healing—
hope-empty
and longing for a
personal sign in their lives,
and we felt panic rise.
How could we feed so many,
so hungry? Where
could we buy enough love?

But one of the crowd, a child,
came forward with
a lunch to share—
just a little—
and you prayed a bounty
and asked us to hand
the bounty out,
feel and smell and touch
the holiness you were giving,
and even taste
the bread ourselves.

And then we gathered up—
so that nothing
that ever was a miracle
in somebody's life
would be lost.
We are not the doers of signs,
but the ones who treasure
fragments—of story
or healing or forgiveness—
who warm them up,
who raise the cup of fish broth,
boiled of prayer and bones,
to lips of crying need,
who break a loaf
already bless-broken
into smaller pieces
that can be swallowed
on the day after.

We are clergy.
We see and encourage
those in our midst
with a gift of lunch or love.
We humbly distribute
God's unbelievable feast.
We are the ones who walk around
after Christ's picnic,
collecting sacrament in the grass
because we remember
hunger comes again,
and because
we love the leftovers.

The preceding materials use readings from the season of Pentecost, Year B.

# Straightening the Spirit's Spine

## (JEREMIAH 1:4–10; PSALM 71:1–6; HEBREWS 12:18–29; LUKE 13:10–17)

### PRAYER OF THE HEART
#### (LUKE)

*"When he laid his hands on her, immediately she stood up straight and began praising God." (Luke 13:13)*

Banish the bent-over spirits:

memory of red guilt or
a long-ago foolish choice;
wrong marriage or
bitter divorce;
small crimes or
little legal brutalities;
a legion of torment
of addictions.
sexual abuse, incest,
domestic violence;
losses of mind, sight,
hearing, mobility;
self-doubt or
its bright mirror—
grandiosity.

Banish the bent-over spirits:

and good things, too;
obsessions now that
began healthy and
twisted a whole life;
professional demands,
creative dreams;
caring for an
ailing, aging parent,
proud-pushing
an achieving child;
beautiful homes

shopped to sparkling,
beautiful bodies
jog-starved to thin;
even the church-work
where faith eats
its children.

Banish the bent-over spirits.

My shoulders sink,
and my spine curls
under the weight, while
my eyes turn in until
I cannot recognize
the one who heals.
See me here,
and call me, Christ.
Lay your hands on
the human meaning
beneath distortion.
In spite of a world
that disciplines healing,
in spite of the people
who do not want
others well,
say the words
that set me free—

that I may straighten into
praise.

## Creative Encounter with the Text for a Small Group
### *Naming the Back-Benders*
#### (LUKE)

Put a broken off, twisted and bent branch in the center of the table, held up with clay. Give people as many strips of paper as they want to write down the things that bend them over (or bend other people over): addictions, emotions, situations, illnesses. Twist and tape these papers into Möbius strips (so that there is no beginning or end), and hang them on the branch. At the conclusion of the study group, put a fragile houseplant in the center. Comment on how moving the strips to the houseplant would physically bend it over and removing them would allow it to straighten up, but that you did not choose to demonstrate such a visual analogy because it might, in fact, have broken the living plant. Sometimes people who are bent do not find a healer in time.

## Suggested Questions for Discussion or Personal Reflection
### (JEREMIAH 1:4–10)

Does God let us hide behind personal inadequacies?
Are there parts of what you are that seem to be "prebirth"—so integral are they to your personality?
What does it feel like to have God's words in your mouth?
When have you been afraid to tell the truth to someone?

### (PSALM 71:1–6)

When do you imagine God as a rock of refuge?
Have you ever been rescued by God?
How is God connected to our birth and prebirth experiences?
Do you think that abortion can be a faithful response to pregnancy?

### (LUKE 13:10–17)

When have you been so "bent over" that God had to see you, call you, and lay hands on you for healing?
What are the spirits that bend us over?
What does Sabbath mean?
Are there rules for kindness?
Why does compassion make us angry?
How do we celebrate healing?

### (HEBREWS 12:18–29)

What terrifies you about God?
Do you come to God with fear or with joy?
What is "acceptable worship" for God?

# Resources for Congregational Worship
## Call to Worship
### (JEREMIAH AND LUKE)

**One voice:** We are invited into the presence of God,
    given words of courage, refuge from trouble,
    healing of memory, forgiveness of sins.
**Congregation:** We are hesitant—
    fearful of being embraced by a blessing
    which is also a consuming fire.
**One voice:** We are invited into the mission of God,
    called to disturb the comfort of others
    and accept freedom and responsibility
    for our own lives.
**Congregation:** We are willing—
    our tongues are tuned to prophecy,
    our prayers are steady even in turmoil,
    our lips are poised to offer God praise.

## Invocation
### (HEBREWS)

We come this morning, O God, not to something that can be touched or counted or controlled, but to your awesome mystery, to the city of the living God, the gathering of angels, and the new covenant of Jesus Christ. We come not in fear but in joy, offering our precious, reverent, and acceptable worship. Amen.

## Time of Reconciliation
### (HEBREWS)
### *Call to Confession*

We come to confession, and it is not fire or darkness or gloom. We come to the living God, judge of all, and to our mediator, Jesus Christ.

## *Confession*

Holy God, we confess that we have not kept ways of righteousness—
    we have fallen short of all of Moses' commandments.
    we have put trust in created things—
        profession, social status, family, nation, church—
        and have been terrified when they were shaken.
    we have not offered acceptable worship—
        our lips have been stiff with our own concerns,
        and our hearts cold from lack of love for others.

8-28-11

We are truly repentant. We pray for forgiveness and
  another chance to seek your perfection. Amen.

### *Assurance of Grace*

Christ speaks words of reconciliation. God's realm will not be shaken. In the
name of the living God, we are forgiven.

## PRAYER BEYOND THE CHURCH

### *Prayer with Women Who Have Had a Mastectomy*

(LUKE)

There are mirrors everywhere.

And we see scar,
loss of beauty, womanhood.
We are relieved, but depressed,
mourning but hopeful,
proud that who we are
is alive and well,
yet ashamed
even with those
we love the most—especially
with those we love.

We are bent over the wound,
our bodies twisted into
a question mark,
asking if we are worth
intimacy anymore.
We are women without a breast,
without two breasts,
without a piece of breast,
always afraid that
cancer will come again.

We are mutilated by our healing.

Before prosthesis
we need love.

When you call us woman,
we are set free.
It is another kind
of healing, and it
disturbs the Sabbath laws
of medicine men.
Now we can straighten up
with our perfect bodies,
perfectly free,
beautiful and naked
like the moon, which,
when it is not full,
is all shining caverns,
shadows of dance.

The preceding materials use readings from the season of Pentecost, Year C.

# Molding a New Life

(JEREMIAH 18:1–11; PSALM 139; LUKE 14:25–33)

## PRAYER OF THE HEART
### (JEREMIAH)

*"Come, go down to the potter's house, and there I will let you hear my words." (Jeremiah 18:2)*

Unfolding God who lives in potter's hands,
you call me into this your potter's house
to catch anew the truths you have to say
and watch you working at the wheel.
Between your hands I see
the rising of your vessel Israel to purity of form,
a pot of holy grace from which
a thirsty world may drink,
but then your turning stops.
In life, perfection tends to spoil.

As does the potter with the clay once thrown—
no matter how sublime the crafting wrought—
when integrity to form is lost,
the vessel is recast.
So, thus, with Israel
you once began afresh.

Unfolding God, who lives in potter's hands,
I come into your potter's house this day
with others—a multitude
of saintly shapes and sizes,
once supremely cast.
We come to set ourselves
between your hands upon your wheel.
Our words and ways have lost their shape.
Our memory of your hands has waned.
The rhythm of your turning wheel
is smothered by our days.

As does the potter with the clay once thrown—
no matter how sublime the crafting wrought—
when integrity to form is lost,
the vessel is recast.
So, now, with me, kind Potter God,
once more begin afresh.

## BIBLE STUDY
### Creative Encounter with the Text for a Small Group
### *Molding Clay*
#### (JEREMIAH)

Give each participant two lumps of clay. Have plenty of newspaper and water. Offer ten quiet minutes for shaping the first lump into a cup, bowl, pot, or vase—something that is useful because it holds something. Set that aside and discuss the scripture using these questions or others while playing with the other lump of clay. Participants can make a sculpture, or just knead, roll, or punch the clay. Save time at the end of the class to discuss how touching the clay and using it for a project and recreation affected the understanding of the text. Let the participants take their creations home.

## Suggested Questions for Discussion or Personal Reflection
### (JEREMIAH 18:1–11)

What is important about human beings—the clay or the shape of the vessel?
Are you destroyed if God reshapes you?
Why does Jeremiah need to go to the house of the human potter before he can understand God's message about change in response to human behavior? (Is it to see that God loves the clay?)
Where do you visit when tragedy overwhelms you?
What can effect change in God's purposes?

### (PSALM 139)

Does it feel like invasion or intimacy to be searched and known by God?
Why won't God let us flee?
Is this a definition of being human: being wonderfully and fearfully made?

### (LUKE 14:25–33)

When does God call us to divide families?
What would be a frightening demand made upon you?
How do you use the word "hate"?
Just how dangerous and lonely is the life of faith going to be?

# Resources for Congregational Worship
## Call to Worship
### (PSALMS)

**One voice:** God has searched us and known us. God has knit us in our mother's wombs and read the book of our lives before our days began.

**Congregation:** We come to worship God, who understands us completely.

**One voice:** God seeks us when we flee—whether we take the wings of the morning or make our bed in the earth, God's hands hold us tenderly.

**Congregation:** We come to worship God, who cares for us completely.

**One voice:** God's thoughts are more than the sand of the sea, yet God knows every word that falters on our tongues and every stumbling path we wander.

**Congregation:** We come to worship God, who loves us until we find ourselves at home.

## Invocation
### (PSALMS)

Gentle God, we are your human children—wonderfully and fearfully made. We gather this morning conscious that your searching has drawn us here to be understood, cared for, and loved. Then, empowered to follow our own paths, we can reach out hands of grace to those who walk around us and with us. Amen.

## Time of Reconciliation
### (JEREMIAH)
### *Call to Confession*

God shapes our lives from the human that is in each of us and molds our purposes out of raw, vulnerable hope. We place ourselves in God's steady hands, so that our lives may be remade.

### *Confession*

Holy God, Potter of our lives of clay, we acknowledge to you and to one another and to ourselves that we have not lived as you call us to live.

We have been centered around the wheel of our own concerns
rather than the needs of others;
we have been molded by our possessions
rather than our possibilities;
we have starved our families for attention or
overwhelmed them with expectations;
we have promoted our self-interest but
have been critical when others do so.

Accept our repentance and hold your hand on our spinning lives to reshape us in your image of love, giving, and openness to others. Amen.

174
*Pentecost*

## Assurance of Grace

The palms of God's forgiveness rest on our shoulders; the fingers of God's tenderness probe our hurt, and the grip of God's guidance leads us into new decisions.

## PRAYER BEYOND THE CHURCH

### Prayer for Menopause

#### (JEREMIAH)

The clay speaks
in the dirty hands of God—

she asks for thumbs
and steady palms
firm against the speed of spinning.

She calls for re-formation
of all that is not centered
being thrown.

She claims her shape—
her own wide open mouth,
a place of long pouring,
a place of deep drinking.

She cries for the time of wheel-rest,
and for kiln-heat,
even for the pain
of something becoming
permanent, hard,
and alone.

And she prays for
the glaze of great beauty and that,
when she knows she is useful,
she may once again
feel around her

the touch of hands.

# PRAYER BEYOND THE CHURCH
## *Prayer with People in Psychological Therapy*
### (LUKE)

It feels wrong, like hate,
to be so honest
about mother and father,
about spouse and children.
It feels like betrayal
and selfishness
and sin.

It feels wrong, like hate,
to claim my own needs
and my own time,
to express my own opinions
and my expectations of others,
to begin a new career
or quit my job,
to want a room of my own
or a vacation alone.
It certainly feels like somebody
is going to call it hate
if I have faith in
something more
than my family.

Thank you for putting it so starkly
it shocked the pray-together
stay-together folks.
I know that finding
who I am
is cross—
not self-indulgence—
and the only way I will ever
balance on my own two feet
to follow you.

I have counted the cost,
and it is high.
I am ready to abandon
all my relationships
for the truth
of who I am—
for I trust that
on the other side of this
vulnerable independence
is the incredible possibility
of new loves and
old tendernesses
made stronger by
my willingness
to let go.

These materials use readings from the season of Pentecost, Year C.

# Hospitality of Home and Heart

## (2 KINGS 4:8–10; ACTS 16:11–15)

### PRAYER OF THE HEART

#### (2 KINGS, ACTS)

*"When [Lydia] and her household were baptized, she urged us, saying 'If you have judged me to be faithful to [God], come and stay at my home.' And she prevailed on us." (Acts 16:15)*

Holy Visitor, holy Guest—
What haunting vision of the night has set you
on the wings of grace
to fly straightway with news of peace
for ears that lean on prayer from open hearts?

Holy Visitor, holy Guest—
What transfiguring light of dawn has set you
on the path of grace that leads outside the gates
beyond the sight of customary ways
for eyes that look to prayer from open hearts?

Holy Visitor, holy Guest—
What restless burning of the soul has set me
on the wings of grace to fly straightway outside the gates
to my long-loved accustomed seat of prayer?

Holy Visitor, holy Guest—
You come to me on wings of grace so like my own two feet;
you walk the path to prayer where I have countless passed,
yet what you say anoints me with a whole new life.

Holy Visitor, holy Guest: I am called Lydia—
I am called by many names.
I wear purple and I pray—
and sometimes I wear green or blue or red or gray.
I have listened; I am opened; I believe.
Take me and mine as one into your fold,

And, then, on wings of grace, both you and yours—
come break your bread from open hearts
in my new and tenderly remembered home.
Amen.

## Prayer of the Heart
### (2 Kings)

*"Let us make a small roof chamber with walls, and put there . . . a bed, a
table, a chair, and a lamp, so that he can stay whenever he comes to us."*
*(2 Kings 4:10)*

God, I want to make a room for holiness.

I will build it on the roof for starlight and the first glimpse of dawn.
I will raise walls to shelter from wind and cold and from the seeing
    of what needs to be hidden.
I will place a bed there for rest and sleeping, and for dreaming,
    and for a place of making alive again.
I will set a table, that we may eat bread and drink a cup of hope
    and tell stories long into the evening.
I will be sure there is a chair for sitting down, for stopping the
    rush of all things, and for praying.
And I will light a lamp to read by and to keep the sleepless hours
    I know will come, and so that, from my lamp-lit rooftop room,
    travelers from distant places can see their way.
I will light a lamp so no one will be lost.

I want to make a room for holiness, God,
    —for the holiness in you,
    —for the holiness I recognize in people whom I love,
    —for the holiness that startles me in strangers.

I want to make a room for holiness, God,
    —for the holiness in me. Amen.

## Bible Study
### Creative Encounter with the Text for a Small Group
#### *Remembering Room*
##### (2 Kings)

Ask each participant to choose one of the following places: a kindergarten classroom; a grade-school classroom; a grandparent's kitchen; a hospital room; a
Sunday school classroom; a church on Christmas Eve; a room in a house where

they no longer live; the greeting room of a funeral home; any room of which they have a distinct memory.

Next, ask group members to remember the details, to imagine themselves in the rooms they picked, and to answer the following questions based on their imaginary visit: How old am I? What am I sitting on? What time of day is it? What is the season? How do I know that? What can I see? What can I hear? What can I reach out and touch? Is there anything I can taste? Am I alone? If not, who is with me? What feelings do I have—joy, sorrow, fear, excitement, peace? If I were to say a prayer in this room, what would I pray?

Ask participants to write the prayers that come to their minds. Suggest that they may want to stay the age of their memory or return to their present age. Encourage them to include some of the details of the senses that they remembered. Finally, share the prayers that the members of the group have written.

## Suggested Questions for Discussion or Personal Reflection
### (2 KINGS 4:8–10)

Do you ever think about "preparing" to have God as a guest in your home/life?

Do you have a place in your home—a room, a chair, a corner, a window sill—which is the place of holiness for you?

What do you do to prepare for guests (be specific, not general: change the sheets, set the table, etc.)?

What are your feelings when you prepare for guests?

When have you been most welcome in someone's home? What made you feel that way?

What can happen in "a room prepared"?

### (ACTS 16:11–5)

Where do you go to pray?

With whom are you most comfortable praying?

Reflect on how Lydia brings together the characteristics usually ascribed to the two sisters from Bethany (Mary and Martha): listening and hospitality.

Does your baptism make a difference to you?

What is the difference between your home and your church?

## Resources for Congregational Worship
## Call to Worship
### (2 KINGS, ACTS)

Come to this place of prayer all you who look to the God of Love for acceptance.

Come and sit down in this room of peace all who turn to the God of Love for courage to change.

Come into this house of grace all who would rise obedient to Christ's will to love without end.

Come into this place through the gates of praise and thanksgiving for God's holy presence.

Let nothing separate you from the love of God made real in you through the life and death of Christ Jesus our Savior.

Come, with open hearts, come; may God meet you with open arms.

## Invocation

### (ACTS)

O Holy One, we come like the Philippians so long ago to a place and a time of prayer. They went out of the city to the riverside, and we have come out of our normal routine to a time of Sabbath in which we can nurture our lives. Rest your gentle Spirit upon us in this hour of solitude and sharing, laughter and reflection, that we may receive the healing or hope, forgiveness or enthusiasm, patience or courage we need for ourselves, and so we can become a place of hospitality in which your good news can be heard by others. Amen.

## Time of Reconciliation

### (ACTS)

### *Call to Confession*

As we listen to the simple story of Lydia of Philippi, we are moved to confession.

### *Confession*

God of the women who walk by the river and pray, forgive us our sin.
　　We do not seek a place of spiritual renewal.
　　We do not listen eagerly to good news
　　　　when it is shaped by new ideas.
　　We do not offer unconditional hospitality
　　　　in our lives, our homes, or our churches,
Open our hearts to stillness of spirit, grace for ourselves,
　　and generosity for others. Amen.

### *Assurance of Grace*

Lydia was baptized and we have been baptized—
　　into forgiveness and the infinite possibilities of love.

# Prayer beyond the Church

*Prayer for Things Purple*

(ACTS)

Gentle God, I give you thanks for all things purple—
    for sunsets and thunderstorm August nights,
    for lupine like freedom blowing above blue ocean,
    for the scent of lilac,
        and the transience of violet,
            and the exotic luxury of orchid,
    for advent candles that burn waiting and hope,
    for a beautiful dress of childhood
        and a postcard from a friend,
    for one amethyst earring,
        an eggplant and a plum,
            grandmother's faded lavender apron
            and satin ribbon tied around a small gift,
    for the common cup of wine like blood
        and the purple taste of holiness in tiny glasses,
    for the color of beauty when I have recognized beauty in myself.

Gentle God, I pray in intercession for all things purple—
    for welt marks on a battered woman's face and shoulders,
    for the smudge under sleepless eyes,
    for wine spilled across spoiled pages of life,
    for the lonely childhood of migrant workers with grapes in their hands,
    for stiff flowers on a sympathy card
        and needle bruises on an old woman's arms,
    for a bridesmaid dress that will never be worn,
        and a half-finished diary,
            and the crumpled metal of a bicycle,
    for the cloak they put on to mock a man with a crown of thorns,
        and vinegar on a sponge
            and twilight by a borrowed tomb,
    for the color of pain when I see myself
      and the color of healing when I do not look away.

All these "purple goods" woven into the fabric of my life
    I lay before you in tender gratitude and urgent hope,
    and ask that you clothe me in the garment of your grace. Amen.

The story of the woman of Shunem does not appear in the lectionary readings. These materials, based in her story, are placed in the summer season. Lydia's story is read on the sixth Sunday of Easter, Year C.

# Fall Ember Days

"In the morning, long before dawn, he got up and left the house, and went off to a lonely place and prayed there." (Mark 1:35)

# The Generosity of God

(EXODUS 16:2–15; PHILIPPIANS 1:21–30; MATTHEW 20:1–16)

## PRAYER OF THE HEART

### (EXODUS)

*"The whole congregation of the Israelites complained against Moses and Aaron in the wilderness." (Exodus 16:2)*

I have tasted my complaining
so long—
opened it up like an Oreo cookie
and licked the filling of it.
I have chewed on bad thoughts
about work and friends,
about parents and children,
about in-laws and ex-spouses,
about illness and wellness,
about imagined slights
and real inconvenience,
about hectic schedules
and empty hours,
about church committees
and the U.S. Congress,
about traffic and weather,
about my prayer life
and my indigestion.

And I have savored them.

Manna me, God.
Manna me a bread so holy
that I don't know what it is
when I first see it,
a daily bread,
which is enough,
and cannot be hoarded

for tomorrow,
a daily bread
of kind words for others
and self-respect for me,
of patience in circumstances
of work and health,
and discretion with
tell-again stories,
of Sabbath for the
busy days,
and prayer for the
lonely ones,
of appreciation for others' gifts,
and understanding of faults—
especially the others
close to me
who are so easy
to hurt.

Manna me, God.
I disgust myself
with my long complaining,
for without your miracle,
I would starve,
turned in on the diet
of myself.

And I am hungry for you.

# BIBLE STUDY
## Creative Encounter with the Text for a Small Group
### *Contemporary Skits*
#### (MATTHEW)

Divide the group into two or, preferably, three groups. Give each group fifteen minutes to develop a contemporary skit that parallels the parable. They should try for the impact of surprise and anger that the first parable must have aroused. Have each group perform for the others. Discuss first whether it was hard to come up with each idea for the skit and then how it was to experience the other groups' concepts. What do we learn from this parable about the nature of God? Does Jesus also intend us to model our human behavior on this parable? How?

## Questions for Discussion or Personal Reflection
### (EXODUS 16:2–15)

Have you ever wanted to exchange an unknown experience for a known suffering?
When do you complain to God?
How does God feed us in unexpected ways?
When have you not recognized the bread of God?

### (PHILIPPIANS 1:21–30)

Do you understand what it is to want to die? When have you felt that way?
What is a life worthy of the gospel of Christ?
What is the purpose of struggle?

### (MATTHEW 20:1–16)

Should a parable make us comfortable or uncomfortable?
When does one person's generosity make others angry or envious?
What are examples of uneven "rewards" in life?
Do you believe that God receives Christians who have come to faith late in life
    with equal love as those who have given many years of service? Does this feel
    unjust to you?

## RESOURCES FOR CONGREGATIONAL WORSHIP
### Call to Worship
#### (MATTHEW)

**One voice:** Come to receive grace—
    all who have been Christians since youngest childhood.
**Congregation:** Come to receive grace—
    all who were converted in adolescence to the gospel's call.
**One voice:** Come to receive grace—
    all who discovered God's hope in the midst of some middle-years' brokenness.

**Congregation:** Come to receive grace—
all who have returned to the church after years of skepticism.
**One voice:** Come to receive grace—
all who seek God only when death appears on your personal horizon.
**Congregation:** Come to receive grace—
all who are deciding today whether to trust God's offer of love.
**All:** God is not partial.
God does not offer salvation by the clock.
God blesses everyone who comes for new life.

## Invocation
### (PHILIPPIANS)

Gracious God, we come striving in mind and spirit to live lives worthy of the gospel.
Touch us with your holy presence which will make
—worship of our jostling words and songs,
—service of our prayers and gifts,
—community of our sitting together.
Open the gospel in our lives so that all may read our faith in Christ. Amen.

## Time of Reconciliation
### (EXODUS)
### *Call to Confession*

Let us enter the wilderness of self-knowing and confess our sins.

### *Confession*

Gracious God, we have complained:
we have longed for the past and distrusted the future;
we have blamed situations on people;
we have become angry when our expectations were not fulfilled;
we have failed to recognize your gifts around us.
Still our complaining voices long enough that we may hear your word of truth.
Amen.

### *Assurance of Grace*

Forgiveness is a blessing like manna—freely, daily given. Gather it, that your
souls may be fed.

## PRAYER BEYOND THE CHURCH
### *Prayer with High School Teachers*
### (MATTHEW)

God, help me teach them all.
God, help me reach them all:

the ones who study,
and those who can't

because violence stalks
their living rooms;

the ones who care,
and those who don't

because basketball
is so much more exciting;

the friendly ones, and
the arrogant ones;
the ones with glazed-over eyes,
and those who are frightened
of things I can't imagine;

the ones who are bright
and look to me for guidance,
and those who are bright
and treat me with contempt;
the ones who struggle
to learn simple concepts,
and those who don't
struggle anymore;
the average students
whose names and faces
I struggle to remember
when they sit
in different places,
and students so bored
by other teachers
they never give me a chance;

the younger siblings
who disappoint me
and make me feel guilty
at my disappointment;
the children of colleagues
I handle so gingerly,
and my own children
whose gaze I avoid
in the hall;

the artist in the biology class,
the surgeon-to-be in shop;
the boys who are too short,
the girls who are too heavy,
and the smooth and popular
and fragile ones, too;

the gay boy and the pregnant girl
who are listening to truth
inside them
more important than my words;

the ones who have night jobs,
and the ones who have nightmares;
the ones who drink too much,
those who do crazy things
in cars and quarries,
and those who don't
ever take a risk
and seem so old
so soon;
the autumn-hopeful,
and the winter-weary;
and all of them in love
in the spring . . .
and sometimes in love
with me.

God, help me teach them all.
God, help me reach them all:

the students in my first year
out of school,
and the students in the
year I retire;
and especially
the ones whose faces
I look into and remember
me when I was young—
beautiful, homely,
laughing, lonely, tardy,
troublesome, tender
students.

God, help me teach them all.
God, help me reach them all.

These materials use readings from the season of Pentecost, Year A.

# Questions That Are Too Hard

(JOB 23:1–9, 16–17; PSALM 22:1–15; MARK 10:7–31)

❖ ✄ ❖

## PRAYER OF THE HEART
(JOB)

*"If I go forward, [God] is not there; or backward, I cannot perceive [God]; on the left [God] hides, and I cannot hold [God]; I turn to the right, but I cannot see [God]." ( Job 23:8–9)*

Labyrinthine God,
I seek you
and I am within you.
I flee you
and you are my barrier.

You hedge me in;
you twist my path
in upon itself.
You hunt me
to the center
place of meaning
where I would not go.

You make my
way longer
through convolutions
of pain and grief.

Labyrinthine God,
I do not understand you;
often I do not like you.
I am lost,
kneeling,
within your
holiness.

## BIBLE STUDY
### Creative Encounter with the Text for a Small Group
#### *Mock Trial*
(JOB)

Job wants to argue with God about his misfortune. God is willing to listen to Job's complaint. Set up a mock trial for God and accuse God of a particular crime. AIDS, the Holocaust, the burning of witches, racism, cancer are all possibilities. Ask two class members to serve as the prosecution and two others to be the defense attorneys. One person, as judge, can determine which questions are out of order. Call the other class members as witnesses to the injustice (because people in their families have suffered or as readers of newspapers). The whole class will be the jury.

## Questions for Discussion or Personal Reflection

### (JOB 23:1–9, 16–17)

Have you ever wanted to argue with God? When? Why?
Have you ever felt like you were seeking God unsuccessfully? Describe this
experience.

### (PSALM 22:1–15)

When have you felt forsaken by God?
Does illness make you feel that God is causing your suffering?
Reflect on this psalm as Jesus' crucifixion psalm.

### (MARK 10:17–31)

Do you believe that possessions are a hindrance to receiving the realm of God?
What effect does your understanding of the story of the rich young ruler have
on your behavior?
How do you understand Jesus' response to Peter that family and possessions
that are lost will be regained in this life?

## RESOURCES FOR CONGREGATIONAL WORSHIP
## Call to Worship

### (JOB)

All who are hunting for God,
all who are angry at God,
all who are arguing with God,
come—
you are welcome to contend
with the Holy One.
Bring your suffering
and your complaining
and your terror.
Come—
God will not hide.
All emotions are embraced
in God's gentle darkness
of power.

## Invocation

### (PSALMS)

Forsaken One, we who have felt forsaken—nameless and lost in a week that
rushed by, bruised and hurt in toxic relationships, empty in grief or suffering
from illness—gather into the community of faith. We are aware that others
have come from times of joy and peace. We who have felt forsaken are blessed

by your holy naming of our pain and by the opportunity to share the reality of our weeping with others who remind us of the possibility of hope. Amen.

## Time of Reconciliation

(MARK)

### Call to Confession

Let us confess the things we place first which belong last, and the things which should be last which become our priorities.

### Confession

Gracious God, we confess—
    that we often identify ourselves and others
      with forms of wealth and good fortune,
    that we are trapped by our possessions,
    that we are falsely convinced of our goodness,
      astonished by your expectations and
      hesitant before any deep commitments. Amen.

### Assurance of Grace

Camels go through needles' eyes.
People give from the depths of their hearts.
For God all things are possible—
    We are forgiven.

## PRAYER BEYOND THE CHURCH

### Prayer with People of Privilege

(MARK)

We are wealthy because
we understand
subtlety,
polyphonic music,
iambic pentameter.
We have causes.
Our Christmas decorations
are not garish.
We are tolerant
and ski.
We teach our children
to appreciate
ethnic diversity,
world music,
and wine.

We are wealthy because
we have appropriate
voices—with
appropriate words
and accents and
volume and pitch.
We swim in comfort
the shoals of such
a wide range of
social settings.
Our cultural instincts
are bred in the bone.
Secure, we speak quietly,
knowing others
will listen.

When Jesus asks us
to give it all—
the money
is the least of it.
You must realize
that our grieving isn't
about the Mercedes,
or the second home
or the clothes
(so casual,
expensive doesn't
need to be
mentioned).
It's not about
first night tickets
or Sanibel vacations.

Any of those
could be sacrificed.

But it's the indefinable
privilege
that won't go through
that camel's eye.
It's the beautiful
good taste, it's the
recognizable,
not-being-quite-like-
those-people,
interior difference
that turns us
grieving away
from following such an
indiscriminate God,

but, then, perhaps you
wouldn't
understand.

These materials use readings from the season of Pentecost, Year B.

# Gratitude and Exile

## (JEREMIAH 29:1, 4–7; PSALM 66; LUKE 17:11–19)

❖ ✄ ❖

### PRAYER OF THE HEART
#### (LUKE)

*"Was none of them found to return and give praise to God, except this foreigner?" (Luke 17:18)*

Grace-filled God,
lover of compassion,
for all who walk
the margins
of this world's
insensitivity,
meet us on the way
to giving up
the uphill road
to hope, when
no one dares
come near.
Hear our calling you
by name.
Hear our confessing you
have power.
Hear our plying you
for grace.

Only you can see us
drawing near,
not as we are
but as we want to be.

Turn us around
in trust
to show ourselves
before your eyes
as whole.
Open us
to feel your power
of love
at work in us
while we are on the way.

Grace-filled, loving God,
when we arrive
in peace at last
where your hope for us
is real—
help us not remember
our differences
but offer thanks
for oneness
in your compassion.
Amen.

## BIBLE STUDY
### Creative Encounter with the Text for a Small Group

#### *Thank-You Notes*
##### (LUKE)

Jeremiah's text is the content of a letter, and the story in Luke focuses on gratitude. Purchase lovely thank-you notes and pass them out—at least two for each person. In a half-hour at the beginning or end of the class, ask people to write words of gratitude to anyone they choose. This is not to be shared, but to give people an opportunity to write in appreciation of things they might not otherwise acknowledge. These could be for recent kindnesses or things that happened long ago. Give all the group members one more card when they leave and remind them to live with gratitude at the core of their lives.

### (JEREMIAH 29:1, 4–7)

When are we asked to pray for the enemy—for someone for whom we really don't want to pray?

Have you ever felt that you had to make a life in a "wrong place"? How did you do it?

What things can you do to improve the welfare of the place where you are?

When do you listen to "prophets" who tell you what you want to hear? Have you ever found yourself telling people what they want to hear?

### (PSALM 66:1–12)

When did you last make a "joyful noise"?

When you are praising God, what portions of your personal history do you cite?

Can you remember a time in your life when you felt God was "testing" you? What happened and what did you learn?

### (LUKE 17:11–19)

How do you feel about the nine lepers who did not return? Why do you think they didn't return?

When you find yourself well after an illness, what expression of faith do you make?

How does gratitude slow you down?

Who is blessed by gratitude?

Have you had experiences of not expressing gratitude to people? What were the reasons?

What would be the effect on you if gratitude were at the center of your life?

## RESOURCES FOR CONGREGATIONAL WORSHIP
### Call to Worship
#### (PSALMS)

**One voice:** Come and hear what God has done—
**Congregation:** God has listened to all our prayer.
**One voice:** When we pass through the torrent of deep troubles,
**Congregations:** God turns the sea to dry land.
**One voice:** When we are tangled in the web-nets of life,
**Congregation:** God does not let our feet slip.

**One voice:** When we are tested as silver is tried,
**Congregation:** God keeps us in the land of the living.
**One voice:** When we go through fire and water,
**Congregation:** God brings us to a spacious place.
**One voice:** Come and hear what God has done—
**Congregation:** God surrounds us with steadfast love.

## Invocation
### (LUKE)

Gracious God,
we come this morning to seek our own faith—
    the faith that makes us whole;
we come to express our common faith—
    the faith that brings us joy;
we come to give thanks for faith—
    the faith that is a gift from you;
we come to share the faith of others and
    offer with love our faith to them.
Receive us into worship with your welcome of grace. Amen.

## Time of Reconciliation
### (LUKE)

### *Call to Confession*

God stirs our conscience into restlessness and heals our very hearts. Let us confess our sins.

### *Confession*

Holy God, we confess that sometimes we are not grateful—
    to people who have cared for us, loved us, and helped us,
    to those who have gone before to give us faith and future,
    to our own bodies for their resilient and patient support.
We confess that sometimes we are thankful in our hearts
    but too negligent or hesitant to express our thanks aloud.
We confess that sometimes we lavish appreciation on others from a feeling
    of personal unworthiness and doubt of our own wholeness.
Heart-healer, Conscience-troubler God, accept our repentance
and plant in us a deep root of gratitude. Amen.

### *Assurance of Grace*

Our return to God is a sign of the healing that already has taken place within us. God forgives us all our sins; thanks be to God.

# Prayer beyond the Church
*Prayer for Interim Times and Chronic Conditions*
(Jeremiah, Luke)

Autumn God, eternal God,
we praise you for temporary things:
    —for the light in a scarlet-edged yellow maple that shines up a twilight hour;
    —for the smile after long sadness that glows from the heart;
    —for the scent of wood smoke or apple cider, a schoolteacher's cologne,
        or talcum on an infant;
    —for the momentary longing to wander when we watch the southward
        vanishing of Canada geese;
    —for the first step of a toddler, the first kiss of a bride and groom,
        the first day awake after surgery;
    —for the fleeting feelings of simple prayer, unconfusing friendship,
        peaceful relaxation, true self-confidence.
For all that is brief and passing and beautiful in our lives,
    for the interim and the insignificant,
    for joyful dailiness and the recognition
    that we must love things that are not forever—
        we are reverent with thanks.

Autumn God, eternal God,
we pray in intercession for chronic sources of grief and pain
and acknowledge that we often give up praying
for just those conditions we least like to hold in our hearts:
    for people who live with illnesses we deeply fear—AIDS and
        Alzheimer's Disease, breast cancer and sickle-cell anemia,
        multiple sclerosis and malnutrition;
    for people who struggle with addiction to alcohol, drugs, eating
        and not eating, gambling—who will always be recovering;
    for people who live with the lifelong challenges of mental illness
        and face its societal disdain;
    for people who feel trapped in cycles of poverty or crime,
        domestic violence or the losses of aging;
    for places in our world whose conflicts have worn down the
        spirits of generations.

Gentle God, we pray that you sow seeds of hope and pour the healing oil,
    then look to us with our prayer-folded hands—
        and open our hands for planting,
        open our hands for stroking—
    in the brief and the lingering,
    in the places we know we will leave
    and those we fear we will never leave,
    in the interim hour and the long season. Amen.

These materials use readings from the season of Pentecost, Year C.

# Whirlwind and Chalice

(JOB 38:1–7 (34–41); PSALM 104:1–9, 24, 35C;
MARK 10:35–45)

## PRAYER OF THE HEART

(JOB, MARK)

*"Are you able to drink the cup I drink, or be baptized with the baptism
that I am baptized with?" (Mark 10:38b)*

Draining the cup,
I have tasted the song
of morning constellations.
Seeking your baptism
I have been washed
by heaven's waterskins.
Reaching for your right hand
I have been sucked
into the vortex
of the wings of wind.

Question me, God,
and ransom me.

Let me feel
your creative violence
and within it
the embrace of
your compassion.
Then I will understand—
in the fiber of my
inward parts

where your lightning
ignites my knowing,
and in my hands
which often close
in fists of resistance
when they are asked
to be slave-hands
for those too familiar
or too strange—
the immense gentleness
of your mystery.

Make known in me
that the power of your
unfathomed divinity—
raw-cloud and flood power
sea womb and
star-boundary power—
is also the chalice
of loneliness,
is also the font
of tears.

## BIBLE STUDY
### Creative Encounter with the Text for a Small Group
*Whirlwinds*
(JOB)

Bring in newspaper and magazine clippings of whirlwinds—tornadoes, hurricanes, tropical storms, nor'easter blizzards. Look at the visual images of power and destruction. Share storm stories. Ask each participant to name a life experience that seemed like a whirlwind. Discuss what it is like to have God talk *out of the whirlwind* or *in the midst* of a whirlwind time. What is it like to be asked to listen in such a setting? Return to the text in Job, and have participants close their eyes and visualize the noise and the visual chaos of a whirlwind while the passage is read once again.

## Questions for Discussion or Personal Reflection
### (JOB 38:1–7 (34–41))

Has God ever spoken to you out of a whirlwind? out of a place of power?

How do you think of your own life and particularly its suffering as related to the rest of creation?

God lifts up wonders and intricacies of the natural order. What is the single most amazing aspect of nature for you?

Do you believe that God hears the cries of newborn ravens?

### (PSALM 104:1–9, 24, 35C)

How was the earth created?

What, in your view, is God's role in creation?

Reread Psalm 104:1–9. What metaphor or simile moves you most profoundly? Why?

How do you imagine that God feels about the extinction of creatures?

### (MARK 10:35–45)

How are leaders servants? How are clergy servants? Should they be more servantlike?

Do you ever seek "special favors" from God? in what situations?

What does it mean to you to drink Christ's cup and be baptized with Christ's baptism? Is it frightening?

## RESOURCES FOR CONGREGATIONAL WORSHIP
## Call to Worship
### (PSALMS)

**Congregation:** Bless God, O my soul.

**One voice:** Wrapped-in-light God,
cloud-chariot God,
wind-wings-riding God.

**Congregation:** Bless God, O my soul.

**One voice:** Earth-foundation-laying God,
ocean-garment-folding God,
thunder and mountain God.

**Congregation:** Bless God, O my soul.

**One voice:** Sower of grass for cattle,
   Stream-bender for the singing birds,
   Cedar-grower, Moon-marker,
   Nest-crafter in the fir tree for all the storks,
   Feeder of roaring young lions
   who return to their dens at dawn,
   Rock-sculptor for wild goats,
   Darkness-holder, Spring-gusher,
   Heaven-tenter, Flame-flinger,
   Caretaker of the people who rise
   in the morning and labor till the setting sun.
   God of all, God of my soul.
**Congregation:** Bless God, O my soul.

## Invocation
### (JOB)

God of whirlwind and morning stars, God who feeds the young lions and the baby ravens, we bring the questions of our lives into your presence and hear you question us. Open us to listen to you in the sacred time of this worship hour and in all our times of reflection on the mystery of your creation. Amen.

## Time of Reconciliation
### (MARK)
### *Call to Confession*

We have wanted to follow Christ on our own terms. Let us confess our sins.

### *Confession*

Teacher and Servant, we confess—
   that we have sought personal glory and positions of prestige,
   that we have connected leadership with power rather than service,
   that we have accepted responsibilities we were unable to carry out.
Please forgive us and teach us your model of servant-love. Amen.

### *Assurance of Grace*

We taste the cup of Christ. We are washed in Christ's baptism. We are forgiven our sins and guided into service.

## PRAYER BEYOND THE CHURCH
### *Prayer in the Last Months of Cancer*
### (JOB)

I was nothing when
you laid the earth's foundation.
I did not measure the crumbled beauty
of its beginning.

I did not dance to the song
of the morning stars.
I was not born
before the oceans

burst in blood and water
salty from your womb.
I do not call the clouds
to tilt the waterskins of sweet rain
and flood the thirsty dust
so that seeds can grow.
I have never flashed
lightning intensity in the sky
or given the child's mind
the sudden fire of knowing.

But I answer your questions, God—
and that is more than
any of these can do.
I answer your questions, God,
and I have not been afraid.

Now answer me—

why was I born to die like this?
why did you bind and loose me
like the constellations?
Why did you feed my youth
when I cried and wandered?
Why did you give me such
knowing and feeling that
rain and earth and sea and sky
are precious to me,
and then number my days
as you number the clouds?

I cannot hunt the prey
for young lions.
I cannot teach them
to crouch in their dens
and walk softly on the
leaves of quiet hunger.
Nor, when the new-born ravens
cry to God and wander,
wing-fragile for lack of food
in the dawn of the day,
can I give the black-feathered
wild glamour of their parents
the reason to fly.

I do not know with your knowing,
but I know with the knowing you
have given me.
I have not been swallowed
in the depths of your eternity
or walked your dimension where
my smallness is not important,
but I am vital with the life
you breathed into me;
and the wild and arrogant voice
of my questioning
is the one you touched
into my throat in an hour
when you were not busy
with the lightning or the desert.

No—I have not entered
the springs of the sea
or seen the gates of darkness.
I do not dwell in the
home of the snow,
or inventory the hailstones,
or lie in the hoarfrost's bed.
I have not carved rain channels
in the desert's vivid barrens,
or breathed an ice wind
so the face of the deep is frozen.
I have not bound the chains
of the Pleiades
or loosed Orion,
or understood the stars,
or held them in my hands.

I am not you, but I am the me
you gave me to be—
my prayer and my curse,
my green eyes and my cancer,
all of me—

I am not answered by your whirlwind,
I am waiting for your love.

These materials use readings from the season of Pentecost, Year B.

# New Covenant and Irritating Prayer

## (JEREMIAH 31:27–34; PSALM 119:97–104; LUKE 18:1–8)

## PRAYER OF THE HEART

### (JEREMIAH)

*"I will put my law within them and I will write it on their hearts."*
*(Jeremiah 31:31b)*

Blessedly assuring God,
Sower of the seeds of life
within the hearts of those
who trust in you,
sometimes I turn my head to you
to find a new way of faith
which makes sense and
bears good fruit;
other times I turn my heart
to feel your loving presence
kindle my willingness
to be a new loving self.

Always I find that one
without the other
falls short of peace.
The seeds of life you sow
are twofold:

a new way of faith to live,
new self of love
to go that way.

Grant me, kind Sower God—
a turn of the head,
a pause on the way,
a catch in the throat,
a brush of the wind,
that I may be yours
on a new way,
as a new self—
in Christ—
watching and
waiting and
trusting in you
again.

## BIBLE STUDY
### Creative Encounter with the Text for a Small Group
*Heart Covenants*
#### (JEREMIAH)

Give each group member three pieces of paper. On the first sheet ask participants in two minutes to write down as many of the Ten Commandments as they can remember. On the second sheet, take two minutes to write the Prayer of Our Savior. On the third sheet (again in two minutes), write all the things they are sure God wants in their lives, or personal times when God has been in relationship with them. Discuss what having something "written on your heart" might mean. What kinds of things are heart-written? Are those things easier or harder to live?

## Questions for Discussion or Personal Reflection
### (JEREMIAH 31:27–31)

What are the seeds of hope in you? How do you know when they are sown?
What is it time to "pluck up" in your spiritual house? to build up?
Are you eating "unripe grapes"? Are they your own, or have they descended to you?
Who writes on your heart?
What are the terms of your covenant with God?

### (PSALM 119:97–104)

When do you love laws and structures?
What laws and structures (even lists) do you love?
Describe an experience of being filled with joy through reading the Bible.

### (LUKE 18:1–8)

Have you ever experienced what it is to "lose heart"?
What does it feel like to pray repeatedly with no sense of having a response?
What does faith have to do with "bothering God?"

## RESOURCES FOR CONGREGATIONAL WORSHIP
## Call to Worship
### (JEREMIAH, PSALMS, LUKE)

**One voice:** Let us worship God, who writes a new covenant on our hearts.
**Congregation:** Let us pray to God, who listens to our cries for justice.
**One voice:** Let us search the Scriptures with excitement and find meaning for our lives.
**Congregation:** Let us rejoice that we know God and we are God's people.

## Invocation
### (JEREMIAH)

God of holiness and life, be in our community as we worship this morning. Reach within each of us for our hopes and longings and help us to express them. Write within each of us your law and love so that we may understand how to live your grace, for we pray through Jesus Christ, who is the meaning of new covenant. Amen.

## Time of Reconciliation
### (JEREMIAH, PSALMS, LUKE)
### *Call to Confession*

Sometimes living a faithful life is as natural as breathing, but often it is a struggle. Sometimes, when we struggle, we fail. Let us confess our failures and our sins.

## Confession

Faithful God, we confess that we often try to be Christians with minimal effort.

We are cynical or despondent about the effects of prayer.
We are superficial or joyless in our reading of the Bible.
We are discouraged when our church is not full of our neighbors.
We are hesitant to express our faith in our weekday life.

Guide us into repentance that calls us to discipline our lives in faithfulness, forgive us when we fall short of our promises, and fill our hearts with your truth. Amen.

## Assurance of Grace

God forgives us and does not even remember our sins.

## PRAYER BEYOND THE CHURCH
### *Prayer with People in Legal Professions*
#### (PSALMS, LUKE)

Bring the Bible
into the courtroom.
Let those of us
who need it most—
prosecution and
public defenders,
judges and bailiffs,
paralegals and
court clerks—
lay our hands
on its binding
and bind ourselves
to truth, justice,
and law.

We are worn down
by the cynicism
and the injustice
and the money;
by false accident claims
and repeat offenders;

by mandatory sentences
for those who
need help rather
than punishment,
and quick paroles
for those who can
work the system;
by foolish civil cases
and broken-hearted
divorces that tear
children to pieces;
by bone-chilling
crimes of violence,
and fraud in the hands
of the most respectable;
by media attention
for one trial and
not for another;
by jury pools filled
with people who claim
being a citizen
is inconvenient.

This is our persistent
prayer—
that once again
we will find law sweet
as honey,
truth clear
as sun-struck air,
justice sure
as struggle.
Justice—not quick
or facile or blind,
not always apparent,
not always full of hope,
not single-sided,
but justice still
to which we can
be faithful—
when we pray and
do not lose heart.

These materials use readings from the season of Pentecost, Year C.

# Taste of Healing, Taste of Tears

(JOB 42:1–17; PSALM 34:1–8 (19–22); MARK 10:46–52)

❖ ✄ ❖

## PRAYER OF THE HEART
(PSALMS)

*"O taste and see that [God] is good." (Psalm 34:8)*

The taste of chocolate is rich,
and bread, crusted,
kitchen-scented and
warm, is broken.
White onions are cut and fried
with garlic and tomato,
laid in corn meal or stirred
in rice and beans.
Lime smells of porch-sitting
all summer evening long
and sweat on my lips
and sand and ocean.
Cheerios roll between my fingers—
a memory of childhood—
and then they crumble.
Pomegranate is sweet
and pink and as strange
as a Song of Songs, and
raspberries in my mouth
burst fire and little stones.
Apple is harvest-red
and not forbidden,

while honey is a slow
and golden joy.
Coffee brews strong
in my nose and mouth
and reminds me
of cold mornings
and long conversations
with those I love.
Yes, every meal is a feast,
even when onions
and people I trust
make me weep
even when bread,
like body,
is broken. . . .

I remember the tastes of God
which are good and many.
You are none and all of these.
I open my lips and taste you—
a prayer.

## BIBLE STUDY
### Creative Encounter with the Text for a Small Group
*Tasty Holiness*
(PSALMS)

Set up a tray of foods; be sure to include Cheerios, chocolate, onions, lime or lemon, berries, apples, warm bread, dates, and a couple things that will help people laugh—perhaps raw potato or prunes. Invite the participants to take one food from the tray and taste/eat it. Let the food trigger memories or images. Out of that reflection and the sensation of the taste itself, have them write a prayer. Share prayers and descriptions of the experience.

## Questions for Discussion or Personal Reflection
### (JOB 42:1–17)

Are you contented with the power and mystery of God when what happens in your life seems to make no sense?

When and why have you felt repentance?

God accepts Job's anger rather than his friends' hypocrisy and glib religiosity. Are true feelings always acceptable to God? Can you hide your feelings from God?

What does intercessory prayer do: for the one who is the subject of the prayer? for the pray-er?

Why do people express more sympathy after a crisis than during it?

Why do you think Job, contrary to custom, gave his daughters an inheritance?

### (PSALM 34:1–8, (19–22))

How does God rescue people from affliction?

David escaped Abimelech by pretending madness, and then thanked God. Do we thank God when *we* are smart enough to get ourselves out of a tricky situation?

What does God taste like for you?

### (MARK 10:46–52)

What do you most want God to do for you?

Why do you follow Jesus?

Do you think of Jesus as being the "Son of David," the heir of the Jewish tradition?

# RESOURCES FOR CONGREGATIONAL WORSHIP
## Call to Worship

**One voice:** We gather this morning for worship, tender with personal concerns and brittle from the bruising of the world.

**Congregation:** We come searching for meaning and hungry for peace.

**One voice:** We pray from personal longings and in intercession for all God's children; we share our hopes and doubts; we offer gifts and celebrate healing.

**Congregation:** May we receive God's unexpected blessings, exalt God's holy name and taste God's love.

## Invocation
### (MARK)

Welcome Healer, Savior, Mercy-maker, Standing-still-center of our crowded lives. Hear our deepest pleas for insight and respond to our need and faith. Do not leave us in our pews this morning, but call us into following you down the roadway of the week to come. Amen.

# Time of Reconciliation
## (JOB)
## Call to Confession

Confession is not a recital of shortcomings and failures; an abdication of responsibility for the results of our deeds, words, and attitudes; or a ritual-magic incantation of purification. Confession is choosing a stance of vulnerability with integrity before God, one another, and our selves. Sometimes we do so with words.

## Confession

God, I repent my sin.
I have come to a silent place before the mystery and power of your presence.
I realize how frail I am and how little I understand.
I have tried to shape with my words things that are too wonderful for me.
Forgive me by accepting my prayer. Amen.

## Assurance of Grace

Our prayers are accepted even as we are stilled in the presence of God. With awe we recognize our incredible value in God's love.

# PRAYER BEYOND THE CHURCH
## Prayer with People in Remission
## (JOB)

The whirlwind in my body
has ceased its fury
for a time.
The family members who drew away
have returned to comfort me
now that I am not in need.
I pray for my insensitive friends—
those who said too much
when I needed a
community of silence,
those who shushed my anger
with their trivial religion,
those who were so
goddamn cheerful
it made God puke,
and those who blamed me
when I was sick.

What I understand now
is that I will not understand.
Death worked in me
to kill death, and
it was called healing.
What I understand now

is the still, wild place
to which I came
after the questions.

My blessings are magnified;
my fortune is more fortunate;
my joys are joyer.
The fields for me are
full of birds;
the days for me
are full of day;
and one day is enough
for anything.

I have been given
more time,
more life, more knowing
of the ordinary ecstasy,
and I swear that the smell
of my grandchild's nap
is all there is
of reality.

Like Job I have been given
three new daughters.

No women are so beautiful
as these, and I give them
the inheritance
of my life.
Their new names* are Hope
and Remember and

Tomorrow—
one who flies,
one who sees the shadows
where death was
supposed to walk,
one who tastes life like
a precious spice.

## PRAYER BEYOND THE CHURCH

### Prayer in a Time of AIDS

(MARK)

My gentle friend,
my precious gifted friend
who could write prayers
that put wings on
the heart
and brushed the soul
with holy color,
jumped out
of the hospital window
after the doctor
who told him he had AIDS
left the room.

Too many friends,
and too much hospice,
too many friends—
I can't count them—
too many tears
in the loving, hurting
begging days.

Jesus, have mercy—
hear me shout
loudly!
This is no
timorous petition
and I won't be quieted—
not by support groups
for living with AIDS,
not by money spent
for education, prevention,
clean needles and
condoms,
not by the

silence-you solace
of ecumenical
healing services.

Quilts are for people
who are lying down.

Jesus, have mercy!
I'm going to shout
even more loudly,
until somebody
says to me
take heart, we're going
to cure this disease.

Jesus, have mercy!
I'm going to shout
until even heaven hears
and you stop in your
God-walking-by
autonomy,
and call me to spring up
shouting—
I know what I want.
I want a miracle,
I want T-cells
and life
for all of us,
and I want to follow you
with my crazy,
passionate, trusting,
irrepressible
well-making faith.

*The names of Job's three daughters—Jemimah, Keziah and Keren-happuch—mean "Dove,"
"Cinnamon," and "Horn of Eye-Shadow."
The preceding materials use readings from the season of Pentecost, Year B.

# New Perspectives

(HABAKKUK I:I–4, 2:I–4; LUKE 19:I–IO)

❖ ⸎ ❖

## PRAYER OF THE HEART
### (LUKE)

*"When Jesus came to the place, he looked up and said to him, 'Zaccheus, hurry and come down for I must stay at your house today.'" (Luke 19:5)*

Journeying, searching God—
Down all the paths of
all the lives of
all the souls of
all of time
you travel.

What is this thing being lost in me
that you know?
I am too short to understand,
for the crowd of things
I pull around me
blocks my sight,
and yet I run ahead of you
and climb that tree
that gives a glimpse
of life to one
too short to understand.

When you come my way,
look up and say—
"Come down with haste.
I am here to stay with you today."

Welcome, kind, searching God—
come through
the crowding fears
and meet my wondering joy.
Come in to save
what's being lost in me.
Come down
my path, my life, my soul
to save one sinner
from an empty-handed self,
to save one sinner's house
from blame,
to save me among others
in heart-hardened distance
from the poor.

Kind journeying, searching God—
Come in our time
and stay so we may feast.
Bind us heart and house
and hand
in love to you,
that we may never be again
too short to understand.

# BIBLE STUDY
## Creative Encounter with the Text for a Small Group
### *Watchtower*
#### (HABAKKUK, LUKE)

These two scripture texts are quite dissimilar. The only common element is that they both describe climbing to a height to gain perspective. "Jenga" is one commercial version of a blocks-game which involves building a tower higher by carefully placing blocks taken from below without disturbing the balance and toppling the structure. Go around the room and have each person take a turn at Jenga (or if you have children's blocks, have each person choose a block and add it to make a common tower). While adding the block, each participant must name something he or she does, or somewhere he or she goes, to gain perspective on life and see new possibilities. What is your watchtower? What is your sycamore tree? And, most importantly, can we have vantage points which we build together?

## Questions for Discussion or Personal Reflection
### (HABAKKUK 1:1–4, 2:1–4)

Have you ever "seen" an oracle?

Have you ever become aware of something that was true for others and wondered what your responsibility was?

What do you see from your watchtower, your perspective, that others might not see?

How do you make things clear for other people—so plain a "runner" can read them?

### (LUKE 19:1–10)

What do you think Zaccheus was looking for?

What extraordinary efforts do you make to meet Jesus?

What did Zaccheus see while up in that sycamore? What did Jesus see from down below?

What does it feel like to come down from a point of observation?

How does welcoming Jesus change how we live our daily lives?

Do you know that you have been (are) lost before God saves you?

Was Zaccheus a detour for Jesus? are you?

## RESOURCES FOR CONGREGATIONAL WORSHIP
### Call to Worship
#### (LUKE)

We climb up through Scripture so we can see God's presence.

We climb down in prayer so we can meet God's love.

We come in to sacrament so we can entertain God's forgiveness.

We come out in offering so we can give ourselves
    to others in repentance and joy.

Remembering Zaccheus of long ago—
    let us worship together.

## Invocation
### (LUKE)

Seeking God, call us down from the trees where we hide and observe. Choose
us to welcome you and turn our lives upside down. Amen.

## Time of Reconciliation
### (LUKE)
### *Call to Confession*

We approach God with our words of confession and with the deeds that prove
our lives are changed.

### *Confession*

Gentle God, we bring before you our sinful selves and our need for reconciliation with others.
    We have done deeds we deeply regret.
    We have spoken words that have hurt others.
    We have trapped ourselves in false expectations, and
        we have accepted transient goods
        to satisfy our deepest longings.
    We have failed to reach out hand and heart to others in need.
    We have been silent when our words could
        have made a difference.
    We have not believed in ourselves
Call us to salvation, God, and help us be at peace with all your children. Amen.

### *Assurance of Grace*

Salvation comes to us. We who were lost are found. We who had too much can
give again.

## PRAYER BEYOND THE CHURCH
### *Prayers for a Time of Disparity between Rich and Poor*
### *Speed*

We run through the suburban streets at dawn
in collegiate sweats and Lycra fashion
so fast we cannot read
the graffiti of desperation
in the city.

We run on the health-club treadmill
and climb the Stairmaster
so rhythmically we cannot read
the illiteracy of the poor.
We run the rat race of the corporate world,
we run the fast lane of the social set,
and, oh, we are always running out of time.

We look for pity when we are run down
and need an expensive vacation,
or when our children run away
and lose our values.
We complain that we have run out of energy
and run over our expense accounts
and that other people are running our lives—
politicians, families, therapists—
and, oh, we are always running out of time.

O God, at the speed of our lives,
we cannot read the call for justice,
even when all around us your broken
vision makes it plain.

### Payback
#### (LUKE)

God, the money of repentance,
four times what we have cheated the poor:

> one time for the education
> that has never been taught,
> one time for the housing
> that is destroyed by despair,
> one time for the crime that has
> tempted the children,
> one time for the drugs
> that have given them nightmares
> when we took their dreams away.

Send some salvation
upon our shattered house.
We cannot buy grace, but we long to buy
the mending pieces for their broken hopes.

The preceding materials use readings from the season of Pentecost, Year C.

# Choosing the Lit Life

## (JOSHUA 24:1–3A, 14–25; MATTHEW 25:1–13)

### PRAYER OF THE HEART

#### (MATTHEW)

*"Ten bridesmaids took their lamps and went to meet the bridegroom."*
*(Matthew 25:1b)*

We watch
from noontime on
the lengthening of light.
While each of us
our separate outward paths
pursues,
inside our souls
we wait
with one desire:
this night
to be a light
for God.

We watch
gold ochre haze
soft-sift vermilion sun
until from pearl-eyed day
pure light like flannel fades.
Our lamps take up the fire.

We watch
our gentle, guileless,
flame-thrown light,
like garland flowers
lily white with hope,
adorn our weary way
with eager confidence.

We watch
for princes' sandaled feet,
for gay embroidered robes

all crimson stuff or blue.
Where are the shining faces,
raven hair, and golden mouths
that seek our light
to tell us God is near?

We watch
our fire's unseen light.
Could God not know we wait?
Footpad sleep steals down the path
to snuff the watching out
just long enough to damp the
short-wicked urge that burns for God.

We grope
disheveled
by the cry to wake
and meet our God
with light.
For those with urge
to spare they quickly rise,
renew their lamp's bold flame,
and set their eyes on God.
For those of us with
no more urge at hand,
no borrowed fuel
can rouse our shrunken flame.
Unless we wake
within our soul
the longing urge of love
that burns unceasingly for God,

our well-intended flames
will lapse each time we wait

and leave our lamps
to stand invisible to God.

## Bible Study
### Creative Encounter with the Text for a Small Group
### *Sharing the Oil*
#### (MATTHEW)

Place a small lamp that burns oil—unlit and empty—on a table in the center of a circle of people. Pass to each one present one smaller vessel (*angeion*) containing lamp oil. As each holds the vessel, reflect on what the oil is that you can add from your life to light the way for Christ to come again. After speaking, each participant should pour a few drops from the vessel into the lamp. When all have added some oil, light the lamp.

### Suggested Questions for Discussion or Personal Reflection
#### (JOSHUA 24:1–3A, 14–25)

What other gods do you serve?
Whom do you wish to serve?
What stands between you and serving God with all your heart?

#### (MATTHEW 25:1–13)

Are you waiting for Christ's return?
When Christ comes again, how will Christ see you?
What part does an ordinary person play in a royal marriage?
Why does waiting often happen when God is expected?

## Resources for Congregational Worship
### Call to Worship
#### (JOSHUA)

**One voice:** In days past, we have lived beyond the river of faith in the one true God.

**Congregation:** Today we come to worship the God who calls us here to a life of faith.

**One voice:** In days past, God has led our ancestors in faith to the promised land.

**Congregation:** Today we come in faith that God will lead us to the peaceable realm.

**One voice:** In days past, our brothers and sisters in faith chose to fear and serve God.

**Congregation:** Today we come in faith into this house to reverence and serve the one true God.

**One voice:** In days past, our forbears in faith cast away false gods and gave their hearts to God.

**Congregation:** Today we are witnesses together, that we choose the God of truth and love to serve.

## Invocation

### (JOSHUA)

People-seeking God, come lead us back into your land of faithfulness. Help us cross the river of our shame for setting you aside. Consider that today we put away the gods we once have served and turn to you in sincerity and truth. Meet us in our intent to stay in relationship with you from this day forward. Most merciful God, we give our hearts to you. Do not cease to seek for your faithful people in this place.

## Time of Reconciliation

### (MATTHEW)

### *Call to Confession*

All good intentions are not sustained to see their promise fulfilled. Bring to God in silence and in shared words, your genuine but short-loved promises to God.

### *Confession*

Gentle Spirit, receive our unfulfilled desires to be your light in this world—
 for the unsent letter to mother, father, grandparent, spouse, child;
 for last year's devotional wrapped in dust bunnies under my bed;
 for the card of sympathy left inside the unwrapped box;
 for the undialed telephone conversation expected by a friend;
 for the canceled reservation to attend the spirit-nurturing retreat. Amen.

### *Assurance of Grace*

Gracious God, your power of love to make whole what we in faith half-start saves us from the agony of inevitable self-defeat. When we come to you in sorrow for our unfulfilled promises, your fingers mend our battered good intentions with threads of kindness from your infinite skein of mercy. Thanks be to God. Amen.

## PRAYER BEYOND THE CHURCH

### *Prayer for Lifelong Companions, at the Time of Marriage or Holy Union*

#### (JOSHUA, MATTHEW)

It's not so much about "I do" and vowing,
as about oil and choice
over the long years.

Gentle One, it's about choosing you
to be God
and not choosing to serve the idol

which is this other person
so precious to me now,
but who would be destroyed by worship;
or serving the idol of love
whose image is so distorted
by society's expectations;
or serving the idols of sexuality
or children or security.
Only if I choose
you to be God
can you guide me
with the one whose hand I'm holding
into the land of promises.

And it's about oil—golden wedding oil,
personal energy and a resource
of gifts and compassion
reserved in a flask I don't share
even when I share everything else—
the golden drops of who I am, and who
I will not lose or spill or barter
so the oil will be there when I wake
to crisis or the unexpected
arrival of a person
I am not sure I love,
and I'll need the wick trimmed
so the light will last
through midnight.

Oil, too, for the lamp
I'll use to walk away
if this relationship divorces,
or for the lamp that will
show a path we walk together
if one of us is ill or changes
in ways we could never anticipate,
or for the walk alone
when death comes
and I lie down to sleep
with all the wise and foolish
hopes and tears
within me, and wait
for the wedding feast
that has no end.

The preceding materials use readings from the season of Pentecost, Year A.

# Unconventional Blessings

(RUTH 3:1–5, 4:13–17; MARK 12:38–44)

❧ ✄ ❧

## PRAYER OF THE HEART
### (MARK)

*"A poor widow came and put in two small copper coins, which are worth a penny." (Mark 12:42)*

When I was proud and beautiful
and my life went well
and I enjoyed my family
and my job, was respected for
being kind, in public ways,
to those less fortunate,
prayed long and meditated,
took care of my body—
ate well and exercised—
kept up with politically correct
language and living,
I knew you were there
somewhere behind glass,
(well, mirror), but I couldn't
touch you, of course,
without some breaking.

When I was so drunk
and sick and smashed
and everybody else knew
my life was smashed,
and I was losing everything
that ever mattered or
seemed to matter to me,
and I looked up to bottom,
that's when I took the two coins
I had left—"God, I can't handle
my shattered life," and
"God, help me be sober,"
and held them out to you.
For a long slow moment
I knew you were there
and I saw you were smiling.

## BIBLE STUDY
### Creative Encounter with the Text for a Small Group
#### Christmas Gift-giving Alternatives
##### (MARK)

This point in the autumn is a good time to reflect on the meaning of Christmas gift-giving. Use the story of the contrast between the widow with her small sacrificial gift and the wealthy donors as an opening. Then discuss and plan a Christmas without "wrapping-paper stress." Share questions like these: What gift has been most meaningful to you? Were you uncomfortable about your Christmas gift-giving practice last year? When and why? What are some alternatives to commercial gifts (handmade gifts, promises of service, donations to charitable organizations)? What does the amount of money have to do with the quality of a gift? What is one thing for each participant that would help the holiday stay more focused on Christ? What gift-giving experiences result in true joy? What can this Bible study group do to help the whole congregation with a more Christ-centered Christmas?

## Questions for Discussion or Personal Reflection
### (RUTH 3:1–5, 4:13–17)

When have you given good advice to others or helped them make a plan for
their lives? What is it like to be a mentor?
What older people have steered you into the future?
What are the strongest bonds between people besides biological ones?
What are characteristics of a "true" friendship?
What is special about a grandparent/grandchild relationship?

### (MARK 12:38–44)

Who are the scribes in our society—the self-righteous who harm the poor?
What makes a gift significant?
What do you learn from watching other people give?
How much are you willing to give God?

## RESOURCES FOR CONGREGATIONAL WORSHIP
## Call to Worship
### (RUTH)

**One voice:** We come before God with our loves and losses,
  with our complicated relationships,
  with our almost-given-up hopes,
  with our long frustrations and unexpected joys.
**Congregation:** Blessed be God who does not leave us in discouragement and
  doubt, but lifts up our hearts through the tender care of others.
**One voice:** We remember the story of an old woman with no children
  and a young woman with no homeland
  and how they cared for each other.
  We look for the unlikely partnerships God has in store for us
  and the blessings which can emerge
  even from our saddest times.
**Congregation:** Blessed be God who surprises us with our own possibilities for
  loving life to the fullest.

## Invocation
### (MARK)

O God, we come with everything that we are and have. Teach us to share not only out of the abundance of our lives but also out of our poverty. Strip our pretenses; still our need for attention; quiet our long prayers. Help us to give away our lives so we can find ourselves in you. Amen.

## Time of Reconciliation

### (MARK)

### *Call to Confession*

God shows us models of behavior in Scripture and all around us in life. We are called to self-evaluation and confession.

### *Confession*

Gracious God, we confess that we are sinners.

We do things that we regret, and we do not even understand why we do them.

We leave unsaid and undone things that would be good for ourselves and kind to others.

We compliment ourselves on our religious behavior and are pleased to be seen doing kind deeds.

Our generosity is carefully measured against our abundant resources. Merciful God, teach us humility, surprise us with forgiveness, and ask of us more than we expect to give. Amen.

### *Assurance of Grace*

God receives our repentance as the first of our gifts. Forgiven, our hearts open wider than we could imagine.

## PRAYER BEYOND THE CHURCH

### *Prayer with Families*

### (RUTH, INCLUDING 1:16)

We who are family praise you
for naming our reality with your blessing—
two women who love each other,
a hometown boy, favorite son,
who marries an illegal alien,
a woman who raises
her grandson,
sexuality across age and
generations,
marriage for security,
in-laws full of tenderness,
and a childless widow
who complains too much.

We who are family praise you
for opening wide even the
house of David,
even the birth of Christ—
to men who love men,
to those who have been
married many times,
or not married at all,
to step families and
foster families and
blended families—
all the Moabite possibilities
of human partnership—
even those that startle
the self-righteous.

We who are family praise you.
We cherish and do not relinquish
to traditional lifestyles
our particular vows,
the vows Scripture writes
for unexpected, unusual,
and unacceptable
relationships:
Wherever you go,
I will go,
and where you lodge,
there will I lodge.
Your people shall
become my people
and your God shall
become my God,
and not even death
shall part us.

(The preceding materials use readings from the season of Pentecost, Year B.)

# Truth and Death and the Reign of Christ

## (2 SAMUEL 23:1–7; REVELATION 1:4B–8; JOHN 18:33–40)

❖ ✀ ❖

### PRAYER OF THE HEART

#### (JOHN)

*"Pilate asked him, 'What is truth?'" (John 18:33–40)*

How many times I do not want
to know the truth:

truth about someone else
when I am more comfortable
with stereotype;
truth about the violence
in my society
which I am unwilling
to see, to change;
truth about my religion
and the anti-Semitism
nesting like snakes
in its prayer;
truth about myself—
the real loyalties
and royalties
that shape my being;
truth about you—
that you couldn't save
yourself then,
and you can't
save us now, and
you are still the monarch
of powerlessness;

and the truth that you love me—
even when I ask
too many questions,
even when I choose
too much Barabbas.

## BIBLE STUDY

### Creative Encounter with the Text for a Small Group

#### *Planning a Funeral*

##### (2 SAMUEL)

Give the participants fifteen minutes to plan their own funeral. Leave the agenda as loose as possible. They may list what people they want to attend or speak, what scriptures they want read, what music sung or played, what they want people to remember about them, whether or not they want visiting hours or flowers, whether they want cremation or burial. Participants can choose to consider their death as happening soon or in some distant future. Spend time sharing what realizations or emotions this exercise brought forward. Suggest that they save this paper to reflect on at another time.

## Questions for Discussion and Personal Reflection

### (2 SAMUEL 23:1–7)

What do you remember about David's life—how many stories? Try to describe David as a complex man.

What are you sure God has promised you?

What lasting covenant have you experienced with God?

When you feel God's spirit speaking through you, what do you say?

What would you like to look back on when you die?

What would you like to have as your "last words"?

### (REVELATION 1:4B–8)

How does God relate to time?

What is the vision of God that brings you comfort?

Who is Jesus Christ in this passage?

Who is Jesus Christ for you?

### (JOHN 18:33–40)

What is truth?

What is the truth to which Jesus testifies?

How do we identify Jesus' realm?

When have God's answers confused you? Have you ever felt that you were trying to understand a situation and God was purposely avoiding giving you clear guidance?

Why did the crowd choose Barabbas?

## RESOURCES FOR CONGREGATIONAL WORSHIP
## Call to Worship

### (REVELATION)

**One voice:** Grace to you and peace from God who is and was and is to come.

**Congregation:** To God, the Alpha and Omega, be glory and dominion forever and ever.

**One voice:** Grace and peace to each one of you who come with your little times—

your memories, your hopes, your doubts,

your minutes of joy and your hours of waiting.

**Congregation:** Thanks be to Christ who loves us and frees us and gathers us together.

So it is to be. Amen.

## Invocation

### (2 SAMUEL)

Holy God, we know that you are not limited by our houses, but rather your love shelters all our worshipfulness. May your Spirit speak through us like the sun rising on a cloudless morning, gleaming from the rain on a grassy land.

May your touch of peace be on our restless souls and your flame of joy be in our lonely hearts, that we may be comforted in sorrows, healed of pain, and kindled with hope. Amen.

## Time of Reconciliation
### (JOHN)
### *Call to Confession*

Let us ask Pilate's question, "What is truth?"

### *Confession*

O God, we confess that we stand with death rather than life.
    Our realms are worldly ones.
    We betray one another and scapegoat those
        who force us to know ourselves.
    We prefer power to authority.
    We do not want to know the real truth
        within our lives.
We repent of our sins and we ask your forgiveness. Amen.

### *Assurance of Grace*

We cannot wash our hands of guilt, but we can be forgiven.

## PRAYER BEYOND THE CHURCH
### *Prayer for Death Row*
### (REVELATION, JOHN)

There are too many truths
in a place where guilt is true
and innocence is true,
and only the truth
beyond the world is real.
There are too many kings—
a king who is law,
and a king who is death—
but the sovereign who matters
is the one who will
die with us.
There are too many times
in a place of doing time,
yet all the time that was
and is and is to come
is holy.

Sometimes guilt is true
and innocence is true.
Sometimes law is strong
and death washes hands.
Sometimes Alpha
weeps, Omega
wears chains,
and the One who comes—
among those who are
pierced and those
who are piercing
offers peace in
wounded hands,
and offers freedom
true as blood
and love.
So be it. Amen.

The preceding materials use readings from the season of Pentecost, Year B.

# *Sources of Inspiration for the Drawings*

## Drawing for Winter Ember Days

This drawing (page 13) was inspired by Betty L. Mayben's 1996 photograph of a bench in the village of Seal Cove on Mount Desert Island, Maine.

## Drawing for Spring Ember Days

The inspiration for this drawing (page 74) was a photograph, taken in 1996 by Betty L. Mayben, of a bench on the Asticou Terraces Trail which leads up the side of Eliot Mountain to Thuya Gardens in Northeast Harbor, Maine.

## Drawing for Summer Ember Days

This drawing (page 131) was inspired by a photograph which Betty L. Mayben took in 1995 at the Blagden Preserve at Indian Point on Mount Desert Island, Maine.

## Drawing for Fall Ember Days

The inspiration for this drawing (page 182) was a photograph by Andrew Lawson of a bench found in the Royal Horticultural Society's gardens in Wisley, Surrey, England. The photograph was published in Mirabel Osler, *The Garden Bench,* one in a series of books entitled *The Library of Garden Detail.* First published in Great Britain in 1991 by Pavilion Books Ltd., it is published in the United States by Simon & Schuster, New York (1991).

# Index to the Prayers beyond the Church

❖ ✄ ❖

# Index to the Scriptures

❖ ✄ ❖

# New Testament